This book belongs to:

DK | Penguin Random House

DK LONDON

Senior Editor James Mitchem
Senior Art Editor Rachael Parfitt
Edited by Hélène Hilton, Clare Lloyd, Seeta Parmar, Becky Walsh
Designed and illustrated by Karen Hood, Hannah Moore, Sadie Thomas
Additional illustrations Kitty Glavin, Rachael Hare
Design Assistance Eleanor Bates, Charlotte Milner, Victoria Palastanga, Rhys Thomas
Fact Checker Sally Beets
Producer, Pre-Production Heather Blagden
Producer John Casey
Jacket Designers Charlotte Bull, Charlotte Milner
Jacket Co-ordinator Issy Walsh
Creative Technical Support Sonia Charbonnier
Managing Editor Penny Smith
Managing Art Editor Mabel Chan
Publishing Director Sarah Larter
Creative Director Helen Senior

DK DELHI

Editor Shalini Agrawal
Art Editor Seepiya Sahni
Managing Editor Alka Thakur Hazarika
Managing Art Editor Romi Chakraborty
DTP Designer Syed Md Farhan
Project Picture Researcher Sakshi Saluja
Delhi Team Head Malavika Talukder

This edition published in 2021
First published in Great Britain in 2019 by
Dorling Kindersley Limited
One Embassy Gardens, 8 Viaduct Gardens, London, SW11 7BW

Copyright © 2019, 2021 Dorling Kindersley Limited
A Penguin Random House Company
10 9 8 7 6 5 4 3 2
013–313910–Feb/2021

A CIP catalogue record for this book
is available from the British Library.
ISBN: 978-0-2413-7557-0

Printed in UAE

For the curious
www.dk.com

MIX
Paper from
responsible sources
FSC™ C018179

This book was made with Forest
Stewardship Council™ certified paper –
one small step in DK's commitment to a
sustainable future. For more information
go to www.dk.com/our-green-pledge

My Very IMPORTANT WORLD

Contents

My world

The world **around me**

People and culture

The **big wide** world

The **natural world**

Exploring the world

My world

Planet Earth is an amazing place. It's also very **big**. And as a small part of the world, you are incredible too! Your family, friends, home, pets, community, and hobbies are just a few of the many things that make up the world and help to make you, **you**.

Our home

Earth is a big ball of rock floating in space, and it's also the planet we call **home**. You and everybody else who has ever lived, is from Earth.

Day and night

The Earth is always spinning. Because of this, different parts of it get **light** from the Sun at different times. This is what causes daytime and nighttime.

The Earth is 4.5 billion years old

Life on Earth

More than 7.5 billion people live on Earth. We also **share** the planet with billions of plants and animals – far too many to count!

Earth's land is divided into seven areas called continents. Each continent is split into smaller areas called countries. There are 195 different countries. Which one are you from?

For someone living on one side of the world it will be daytime at the same time it is night time for someone on the opposite side.

The blue planet

Earth is sometimes called the "blue planet" because of the way it looks from space. Earth looks blue because most of it is covered in **water**.

Although we may speak different languages, eat different food, and have different beliefs, most people have a lot in common with each other.

People live in huge bustling cities, tiny villages, rural towns, and everywhere in between.

Who am I?

Each person on Earth is different – and that's a great thing! It's these differences that help **make us who we are**. But we all have plenty of things in common, too!

Personality

Are you loud and adventurous, or more quiet and creative? The **way you act** makes you, you.

Appearance

Are you tall or short? Do you have short brown hair or curly blonde hair? Your looks are only a **tiny part** of who you are.

Beliefs

Is there anything you **feel strongly** about? Are you religious? People believe in many different things.

Home life

Where you live and what you learn will have an impact on who you will be in the **future**.

Hobbies

Are you a football fanatic, a bookworm, or a mathematician? What **interests** do you have that are special to you?

Experiences

The things that have happened and will happen to you – your experiences – might make you **look at the world** in a different way from your friends.

Family

What's **your role** in your family? Are you a big sister, a little brother? Or perhaps you're an only child.

Family history

You won't have met them, but your ancestors have **changed your life** – in fact, you wouldn't be here without them!

What makes me, me?

Part of who you are is down to **nature** (the things you are born with), and some of who you are is down to **nurture** (things you experience as you grow up).

Seeing double

Even though they look the same, identical twins have their own **personalities** and can be totally different people like everybody else.

Identical twins share the same genes.

Nature

Nurture

Features like your eye colour and height are already fixed before you are born. They are **natural** and can't be changed.

Most things about you aren't decided before you are born. Everything you **learn** and **experience** in life will shape you as you grow. Your family, teachers, and experiences will all have a big impact on your life.

Genes

Everybody is born with genes that **carry important information** about them, including how they'll look. We get our genes from our parents.

One of a kind

Brothers and sisters often have the same parents, live in the same house, eat the same food, and follow the same rules, but they can have very **different personalities** and might not be at all alike when they grow up.

My body

Our bodies are incredible machines with incredible parts. **Organs** are very special parts that do important jobs to make our bodies work.

The **brain** is like the body's computer. It tells other organs what to do, and is responsible for things such as memory, speech, and thought.

Nerves aren't organs, but the brain uses them to send messages around the body. They let us know if things feel hot, cold, painful, or even ticklish!

Brain

Heart

Stomach

Lung

The **skin** is the biggest organ. It wraps around the body and has lots of jobs, including protecting us from harmful substances.

The **heart** pumps blood around the body, the **lungs** help us breathe, and the **stomach** and other organs turn our food into energy our bodies can use.

The kidneys, liver, and intestines are all important organs, too.

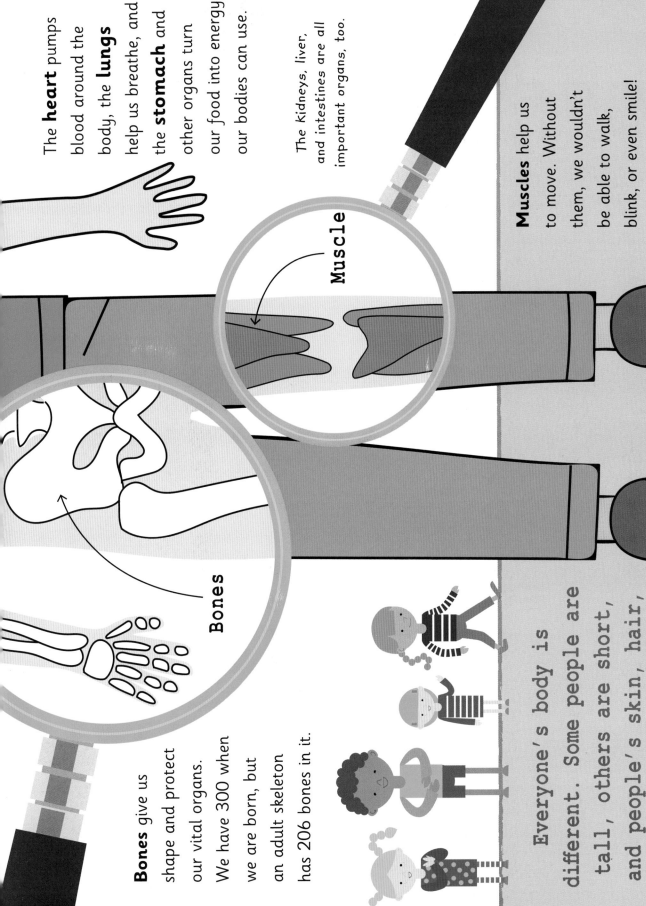

Muscle

Bones

Bones give us shape and protect our vital organs. We have 300 when we are born, but an adult skeleton has 206 bones in it.

Muscles help us to move. Without them, we wouldn't be able to walk, blink, or even smile!

Everyone's body is different. Some people are tall, others are short, and people's skin, hair, and eyes can be lots of different colours.

My brain

Snug inside your head is your brain. Your brain **controls** the rest of your body, and helps you to think and do all sorts of amazing things.

Logic

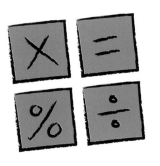

Maths

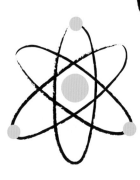

Science

Speech

Brain workout

When you exercise, **blood carries oxygen** to your brain more quickly. Studies show this makes your brain work better!

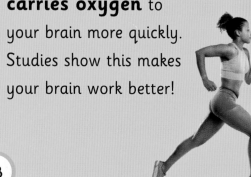

The brain helps you:

Think

Touch

See

Remember

Understand

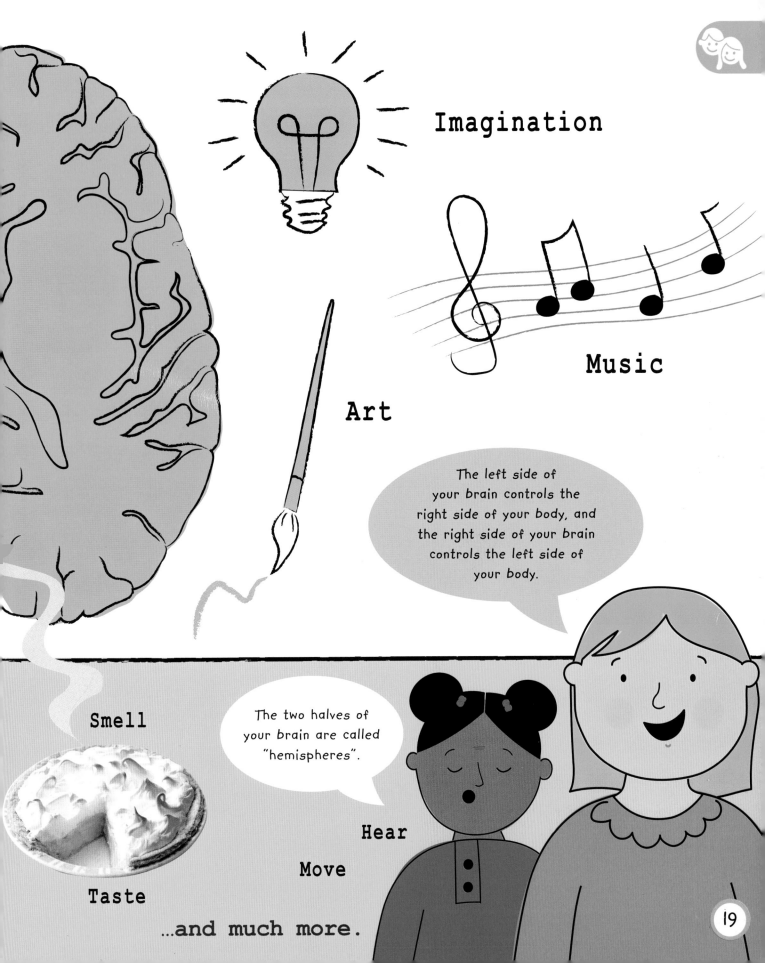

Healthy me

It's important to keep your body **healthy**. Eating well, drinking water, keeping clean, and getting enough sleep are good ways to do this.

Keep moving

Exercise is good for your body and your brain. Want to feel good? Go outside and play!

Yoga helps me relax and is good for my body.

Aaand relax...

It's normal to feel worried or stressed sometimes. **Take a break** and do something you love, like talking to friends or playing fun games.

Your body is your home for life, so look after it!

Freshen up

Wash away dirt and germs from your body and clothes for a **cleaner** and healthier you.

Health helpers

Doctors, nurses, and dentists help you look after yourself. Dentists help you care for your teeth, while doctors and nurses care for your mind and body.

Eat your greens

Eating fruit and vegetables will help you fight off illness and give you more **energy**.

Drink water

Your body is mostly made of water. Be sure to drink enough to **replace** what you lose during the day.

Stroking pets can keep you calm. Purrrfect!

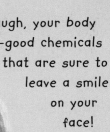

Laughing is good for you!

When you laugh, your body releases feel-good chemicals that are sure to leave a smile on your face!

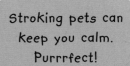

Hip hip hooray!

Which of these emotions do you recognize? What makes you feel that way?

Calm

Confused

Angry

What am I feeling?

Emotions are made in your brain and affect you in lots of ways. Some feel good, others hurt, but every **emotion** is important. Try to listen to how you feel!

Show your emotions

Emotions can **build up inside you** slowly over time, and other people might not realize how you feel. Whatever you are feeling, it's good to talk and share your thoughts with people you trust.

Surprised

Frightened

Excited

Worried

We often feel many different things all at once. Your brain is amazing so emotions can be complicated!

Embarrassed

I write and draw my feelings in a diary.

Feelings

It isn't always easy to tell others how you feel. If you find it hard to put your emotions into words, you could **draw** or write about how you feel.

Body language

Often you can tell how a person feels by watching them move or by seeing the **look on their face**. This is because you recognize your own emotions in other people.

Facing your fears

We all get scared sometimes. It feels terrible, but fear can be useful. Fear is really just our body's way of keeping us out of **danger**.

Why do we feel fear?

When faced with something scary, our body reacts by making our heart beat faster and our lungs breathe harder. This prepares us to either fight off the threat, or run away. This is an **instinct** called "fight or flight".

Some people are very scared of something

Here are some common phobias:

Arachnophobia
(Fear of spiders)

Didaskaleinophobia
(Fear of going to school)

Nyctophobia
(Fear of the dark)

Ophidiophobia
(Fear of snakes)

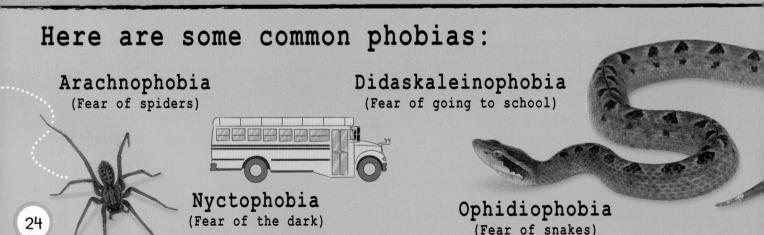

Even the bravest people get scared sometimes. Being brave means overcoming your fears.

Talking to a grown-up you trust can help make your fears less scary.

in particular. This is called a **PHOBIA**.

And some more unusual phobias:

Arachibutyrophobia
(Fear of peanut butter sticking to the roof of your mouth)

13

Koumpounophobia
(Fear of buttons)

Sesquipedalophobia
(Fear of long words)

Triskaidekaphobia
(Fear of the number 13)

Family and friends

There are many **different types of family**. Some families are very large, while others only have two people.

Many families live together, but not all do.

I live with my mum, dad, sister, and our dog.

My family is very big. I have one brother and four sisters.

We were adopted and have two dads.

I have a big extended family. My grandparents live with us.

What is your family like?

We are best friends!

Friendship

Friends are the family you **choose**. You might have one close friend, many friends, or lots of smaller groups of friends. You can turn to your **friends** if you ever need help.

I live with my mum during the week and my dad at weekends.

We've just become a family of three!

Homes

Your home is the place where you live. We should all feel **safe** and happy at home.

Houses

Many people live in a house. Houses come in lots of shapes, and can be **big or small**. Some people live alone, and others live with friends or their family.

Home, sweet home!

Flats

Big cities don't always have room for lots of houses, so people live in flats. A flat is a small part of a **larger building**.

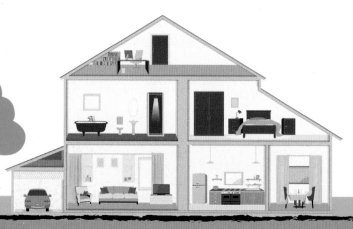

Buckingham Palace

One of the most famous homes in the world is Buckingham Palace in London, England. It's the home of the British Royal Family.

Buckingham Palace has 775 rooms!

City life

Cities and towns are **bustling**, lively places. There are often more jobs in the city, as well as shops, museums, theatres, cinemas, and restaurants for people to enjoy.

Country life

If you love **nature** and **fresh air**, then the countryside is a great place to live. There's more space in the country, as well as more trees and animals.

Life on Mars

Could humans ever live on a different planet? Astronauts are hoping to travel to Mars to study the Red Planet.

Mars ⌒

The first homes on Mars might be inflatable tents covered in ice.

chirp chirp

Cheep cheep

Perfect pets

From cuddly cats and playful puppies, to scaly snakes and brightly coloured birds, all pets need plenty of **love and care**.

Budgerigars

Blue, yellow, white, or green, these feathery friends are a colourful bunch who love to whistle and chirp.

Cats

While these furry felines love to explore and play, they also enjoy curling up in a cosy spot and taking a nap.

Rabbits

Take care of these long-eared pets with plenty of hay, water, lots of space, and a rabbit friend. They'll reward you by hopping over for a stroke.

Horses

With shiny coats, thick manes, and long tails, it's easy to see why people love horses and ponies. They need lots of attention and plenty of space to gallop around.

Snakes

Many snakes are dangerous but most pet snakes are harmless. You only need to feed them about once a week.

Is your favourite pet CUTE and CUDDLY,

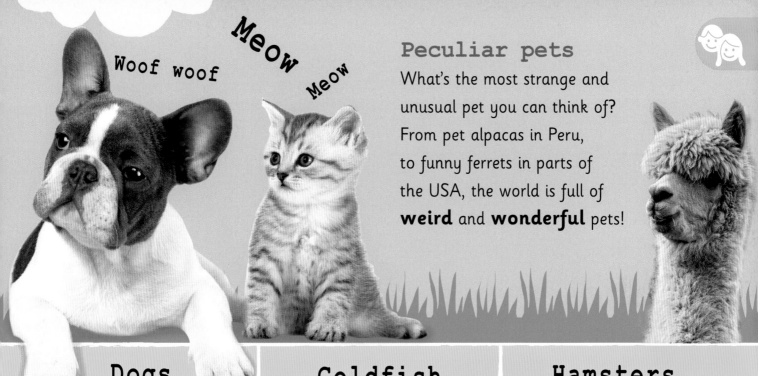

Woof woof

Meow Meow

Peculiar pets

What's the most strange and unusual pet you can think of? From pet alpacas in Peru, to funny ferrets in parts of the USA, the world is full of **weird** and **wonderful** pets!

Dogs

It's no surprise dogs are one of the most popular pets in the world. These lovable canines are friendly, loyal, and great company.

Goldfish

These scaly fish are easy to look after. Sprinkle a few flakes of food for them and watch as they swim up for a snack.

Hamsters

With silky soft fur and lots of energy, hamsters are popular little pets. They are often found scurrying around their cages in the middle of the night!

Lizards

These reptiles can be patterned or have beautiful coloured scales. Many can fit in the palm of your hand!

Spiders

While many people are scared of spiders, they make a good pet for others. They don't make noise and don't need much space.

Tropical fish

Big, small, spotty, or stripy, tropical fish bring a splash of pattern and colour to any home.

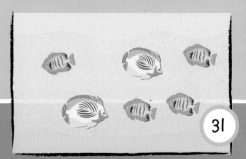

or SCALY and SLITHERY?

The world around me

Even as you read this book, the world around you is **changing**. That means there are always new things to learn, new people to meet, and new places to discover. As you explore your world, you will change too, and grow more amazing every day.

Telling time

Everything we do, such as eating a meal or playing a game, takes a bit of time. That's why it's important to **keep track** of it. What are you going to do today?

Time is measured the same way everywhere, otherwise it would be confusing! We count time using seconds, minutes, hours, and days.

Daily routines

Most people do similar things every day, and wake up, eat breakfast, go to school, play, and go to bed at the **same time** most days. This is called a daily routine. What's yours?

Seconds: Slowly say "one" out loud. That's about one second.

Minutes: There are 60 seconds in a minute. You should spend two minutes brushing your teeth.

Hours: There are 60 minutes in an hour. Lunchtime might take about an hour.

Days: One day and one night take 24 hours.

How to use a clock

These lines around a clock each represent one minute.

The long hand moves around to tell us how many **minutes** of the hour have passed.

The short hand moves around the clock to tell us how many **hours** have passed.

When the long hand points straight **up**, it marks the hour. We call this **o'clock.**

If the short hand is pointing to 7, and the long hand is pointing up, it's 7 o'clock.

Digital clocks

Many clocks show the time using numbers instead of hands. Both clocks say it is 7 o'clock.

Time zones

Earth is split into time zones, and it is **not the same time everywhere at once**. When you eat breakfast, people on the other side of the world will be eating their dinner at the same time!

The calendar

Remembering important **dates** like your birthday is much easier with a calendar. Calendars keep track of days, weeks, months, and years.

Days and months have different names to help us keep track.

Months

January
February
March
April
May
June
July
August
September
October
November
December

Days

Monday
Tuesday
Wednesday
Thursday
Friday
Saturday
Sunday

Calendars help us plan what we're going to do.

We use seconds, minutes, and hours to plan our days, but we need bigger measurements of days, weeks, months, and years to plan longer periods of time.

Days

There are 24 hours in a day. A day is how long it takes for the Earth to spin around once.

Weeks

A group of seven days is called a week.

Months

Not all months are the same length. They have either 30 or 31 days, except February, which has 28 or 29.

October

Monday	Tuesday	Wednesday	Thursday	Friday	Saturday	Sunday
		1	2	3 School concert	4	5
6	7	8 Football practice	9	10	11	12
13	14	15	16	17	18	19 Visiting Grandma
20	21 Piano lesson	22	23	24	25	26
27	28	29	30 My birthday!	31		

Years

A year is how long it takes for the Earth to orbit (travel around) the Sun. There are 365 days in a year. This is the **same** as 52 weeks or 12 months.

Calendars are useful for remembering important dates like your birthday!

Going to school

All around the world, children go to school. Schools teach pupils **important skills** that will help them when they grow up.

School uniform	Lessons	Teachers
Many children go to school in their own clothes, but others have to wear a special **school uniform.**	**Maths, English**, and **science** are just a few subjects taught in schools. You'll learn all sorts of useful topics during the school day!	Teachers have a very important job! They **help students to learn** and understand one or many different subjects.

I'm allowed to wear jeans to school.

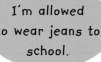

I have to wear school uniform.

Teachers help you when you get stuck!

Getting to school

Some children travel by car, bus, train, bike, or on foot – there are **many ways** to get to school!

Some places have special buses for school children.

School dinners	After school	Back to school
Some children take a tasty **packed lunch** to school, while others eat in the **school cafeteria.**	Many children are given work to do after school. This is called **homework**. Some children go to **after-school clubs**.	It isn't just children that go to school! Many **adults** go to classes to improve their skills or to help them learn new ones.

School dinners vary depending where in the world you are.

Some children play sports after school.

I've gone back to school!

Some children write on chalkboards.

39

Schools
of the world

Schools in different places do things a little differently, but every school wants its children to get a good **education**.

Some pupils have to walk for miles to get to school.

USA
School sports are an important part of American culture.

Brazil
Many schools close at lunchtime so children can go home and have lunch with their parents.

I go to school in Pakistan. Not all my friends get to go to school.

Chile
In Chile, children have a long three month break from school every year.

A helping hand

Some charities raise money to build schools and train teachers in places where many children aren't able to go to school.

School in Argentina

In Finland we don't start school until we are seven.

China
Children in China stand to attention when their national anthem is played at school.

South Korea
From 2019, computer coding is being taught in Korean primary schools.

Shodo

Japan
Almost all children in Japan go to school. As well as subjects like maths and science, students learn traditional Japanese arts like shodo, a form of calligraphy.

School in China

India
City Montessori School in Lucknow, India has more than 55,000 students. That's the most of any school in the world!

South Africa
Grown-ups are working hard to try and make sure all children get a primary education.

School in Tanzania

I work hard at school and like seeing my friends.

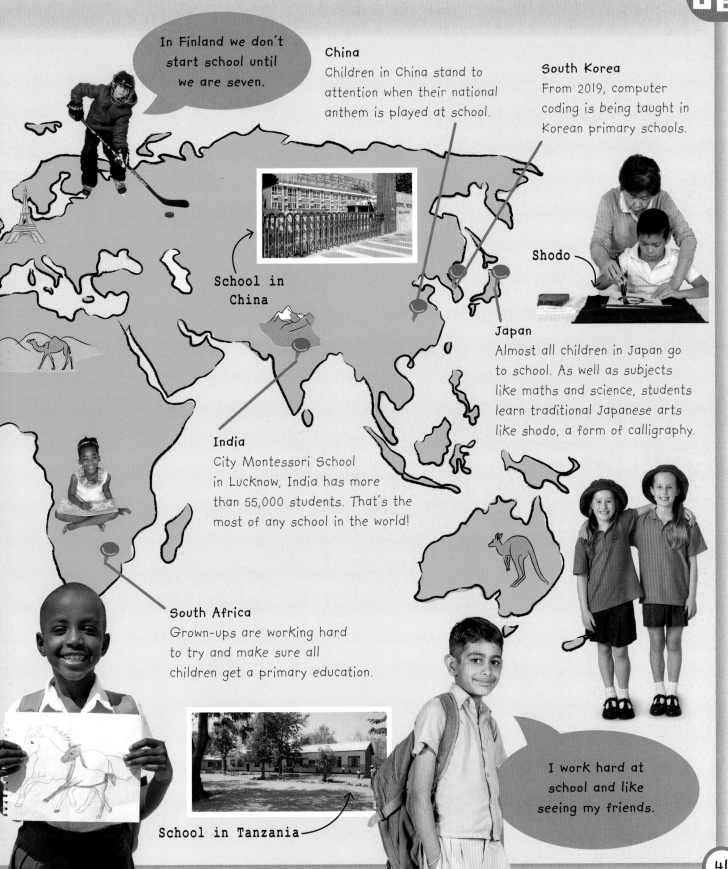

The world of **work**

Working hard is important, so it's lucky there are lots of **amazing jobs**!

> I'm an astronaut. My job is out of this world!

What do you want to be when...

Engineer

Designing, building, and fixing **machines and structures** are just a few things you might do as an engineer.

Astronaut

Ever wondered what it feels like to **race into space** in a rocket? Become an astronaut and your dream could become reality!

Mars Rover

Vet

Do you love animals? Do you want to help **poorly pets** get better? Study science, learn about animals, and you can.

Writer

Want to write the next bestseller? **Grab a pen** and paper, and start scribbling.

Scientist

As a scientist you can create life-saving medicines, amazing inventions, or work out ways to **help the planet**.

Farmer

If you like early mornings and long days **working outside**, being a farmer who raises animals and grows food might be ideal.

Farmers grow much of the food we eat.

...you grow up?

Performer

Do you love acting, singing, dancing, and being the star of the show? Then you could be an **entertainer**.

Designer

Do you have a passion for fashion or an **eye for style**? If so, the life of a designer might be your true calling!

Builder

Fancy **building a house** fit for a queen? Grab your gear and head to the construction site!

Pilot

Want a job with a great view? As a pilot you'll spend loads of time in the clouds and **travelling the world**.

Athlete

Are you a speedy sprinter, a talented tennis player, or a **superb swimmer**? Being a top sports person takes years of hard work but you might become the **best of the best**!

Emergency services

Many people **work hard** to care for others. It's their job to keep us **safe** and **healthy**.

Helicopter rescue

Coastguard

If someone needs help at sea, coastguards jump on board a **lifeboat** and rush to help. Air ambulance crews are similar, but they help from a **helicopter**.

Paramedic

Paramedics treat sick patients at the scene of an accident, before racing them to hospital in an **ambulance**.

Doctor

It takes years of **training** to become a doctor. They make sure sick or injured patients are given the right **treatment** to get better.

My favourite teammate is Snoop the sniffer dog. We work together to catch criminals!

I love looking after patients.

You need to be fit to be a firefighter.

I use my nose to find clues and help the police!

Nurse

Helping doctors and **caring for patients** can be tough but rewarding for nurses.

Police officer

It's important to make sure people **feel safe**. Police officers have the power to arrest law breakers.

Firefighter

Firefighters keep people safe and **out of danger** by racing to emergencies in **fire engines** and putting fires out.

Staying safe

The world can sometimes be a **confusing** place. It's important to know how to stay safe and what to do in an emergency.

Emergency!

If there's an accident you might need to **call for help**. Ask your parent or carer what number you need to call for the emergency services.

It's ok to give your name to the emergency services. It's their job to help you.

An ambulance will help if you or someone else is badly hurt.

The police will be able to help if you've seen a crime.

The fire service will help if there's a fire or someone needs rescuing.

IMPORTANT: Only call the emergency services if there is a real emergency.

Stop, look, and listen!

Always look both ways a few times before you cross a road.

Stick together

Never wander off on your own. If you accidentally lose the person you're with, don't panic – they're probably close! If you can't see them, stay where you are and tell an adult what's happened.

Stranger danger

Don't accept a lift or food from anyone you don't know, and don't open the door to strangers if you're at home by yourself.

Adults you can trust

• Teachers
• Doctors
• Police officers
• Firefighters

Ask a parent or carer to help you think of more adults you can trust.

Stay safe online

The Internet is great, but there are also unhelpful things online and it isn't always easy to tell what is okay. If you're unsure about anything you see, speak to a grown-up straight away.

Talk about it

If you're worried, upset, or confused about anything that has happened to you, tell someone! The adults you trust won't mind, they want to help you and keep you safe!

Bullying is...

It can be hard to describe, but if you have ever been picked on, been left out, or frightened by someone, you know **how bullying feels.** Bullying is all these things and more:

Pinching

Name calling

Laughing at someone

Embarrassing someone

Leaving someone out on purpose

Teasing

Telling tales about someone

Kicking

...or any other way to pick on someone that makes them feel sad.

Help!

If you are being bullied, you are not alone. Lots and lots of people have been through it too. There are many people who want to help you. Tell grown-ups at home and at school until it stops. **Bullying is never normal or okay.**

Why do people bully?

People who bully often feel **sad, lonely, and powerless**. They are often bullied themselves by someone else. They hurt others to be noticed. Children who bully often don't know how to make friends. If you can, try to show them how to play nicely.

Be a superhero

You can be a **superhero by standing up to bullying**! The best way to do that is to speak up and tell a grown-up straight away. If you know someone is being bullied, try to look after them.

Bullying online is called cyberbullying. It's just as bad as other types of bullying.

Who you are doesn't change when someone treats you badly. You are always amazing!

49

Food

We need food to make us go. Eating a **balanced diet** will give you energy, help you grow, and keep your body healthy.

Banana →

Broccoli →

Mushroom →

Sweetcorn →

Broccoli, kale, and other **vegetables** are packed with healthy goodness. Make sure to eat your greens!

Onions →

Apple →

Cherry →

Strawberry →

Raspberry →

Apples, oranges, and other **fruits** help keep our skin healthy and help food to pass through our bodies. They're a great healthy snack.

Kale →

Tomatoes →

Potatoes →

Vegetarians are people who choose not to eat meat.

Orange →

Rice →

Watermelon →

Grape →

Pasta

Starchy foods such as potatoes, rice, and bread, are called **carbohydrates**. They are our bodies' main source of energy.

Bread →

Cheese, milk, and yoghurt are **dairy** products. They contain calcium, which helps to keep your teeth, nails, muscles, and bones strong and healthy.

← Cashews

← Walnuts

Meat, beans, eggs, and nuts are high in **protein**, which helps your body to grow and repair itself.

Prawn

← Butter

Yoghurt

Cheese

Lentils

Egg

Beans

Olive

Avocado

Fish

Chicken

Healthy **fats**, like those in olives and avocados, help our bodies absorb vitamins. We shouldn't eat too many unhealthy fats and **sugars**, like those found in sweets and bacon.

Sweets

Food around the world

Every country in the world has its own tasty food and **traditional dishes**. It's a lot of fun to try exciting new dishes and discover new favourites.

Paella

Paella is a famous rice dish from **Spain**. Almost every country in the world eats rice, but in some places it is eaten with every meal.

Scientists have invented meat-free burgers that taste almost like the real thing.

Grated cheese adds seasoning and flavour to pasta dishes.

Pasta

There are hundreds of different types of pasta! Each pasta shape is designed to go perfectly with certain sauces.

Sushi

This delicate **Japanese** dish is made with sticky rice and often fresh, raw fish. It's so pretty, it looks like a work of art!

Pies can have a sweet or savoury filling.

Tacos

This **Mexican** dish is made with corn or wheat flatbreads. They are served with beans, meat, seafood, vegetables, and toppings.

Pizza

Pizza was invented in **Italy**. Bread is topped with tomato sauce, cheese, and sometimes other ingredients, then baked in a very hot oven.

Greek salad

Olives are an essential part of this summery salad. They grow in sunny groves across **Greece** and can be squeezed to make olive oil.

Kimchi is a Korean dish of spicy pickled cabbage.

On the farm

Do you ever wonder where the **food on your plate** comes from? Most of what you eat has been grown on a farm.

Animals on a farm

Pigs, cows, and chickens are raised for meat, but some animals are also kept to produce milk or wool.

We frighten birds away from planted seeds.

Scarecrow

Sheep

Tractor

Cow and goats are kept for milk.

Cow and calf

Goat

Chickens

Hens are female chickens. They lay eggs that chicks can hatch from.

FREE-RANGE chickens have space to run around instead of being shut in a barn.

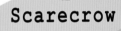

Farmers use machines, such as tractors and harvesters, to help on the farm.

Combine harvester

Dogs can be trained to help the farmer look after the other animals.

Lambs

Baa!

Sheep fur is used to make wool.

Piglet

Plants on a farm

The plants we grow for food are called **crops**. There are lots of types, but these are some of the main ones:

Wheat is a type of grass that is used to make flour and turned into bread and cakes.

More rice is grown than any other crop. Almost half the world's people eat it daily.

Corn is also known as maize. It can be eaten on the cob or used as an ingredient in lots of other foods.

Carrots are grown underground in long rows. They're orange now but used to be purple!

Soy beans can be used to make soy milk and tofu. They are also grown to make food for animals to eat.

Sugarcane is grown in hot places. It's converted into sugar and tastes very sweet.

Help the planet

There are lots of ways to help **look after our planet** so people in the future can enjoy it, too. Planet Earth needs your help!

Use clean energy

Humans burn fuel to make the energy that powers our cars, factories, and homes. However, this releases harmful things into the air. Instead, we can use **clean energy**, such as wind power or sunlight.

Wind farm

Solar panels

Be a forest friend

Forests are very **important**. Trees clean the air we breathe and provide homes for lots of animals. But many forests are being cut down to make room for cities or farms, or to be turned into wood and things like paper that can be sold. We should buy from companies that are environmentally friendly.

How can I help?

- Eat more vegetables and less meat.
- Save energy by turning off switches and lights.
- Always put your rubbish in the bin and sort your recycling.
- Walk or cycle instead of driving to school if you can.
- Tell other people how they can help the planet too!

Protect animals

There are millions of different kinds of plants and animals in nature, but many are in danger of disappearing. Animals such as leopards, gorillas, pandas, and tigers are running out of places to live. Protected nature reserves give animals a **safe home**.

Leopard   Gorilla

The rubbish problem

Humans make lots of rubbish, which can end up in the wrong place, like the ocean! Lots of it, such as paper, cardboard, some metals, and some plastics can be **recycled**. That means instead of going to waste, they are saved and turned into something new.

Reusable bags and cups help cut down on plastic waste.

57

Technology

Imagine life without cars, computers, or phones… All this technology had to be **invented** before we could enjoy it.

Let's talk tech

Technology isn't just cool gadgets, it's everywhere and we use it every day. Your bike is technology, and so are medicines, photos, the machines that power cities, and loads more.

Satellites orbit Earth. They take photos from space with huge telescopes.

Computers are getting cleverer all the time. Some can even be controlled with your eyes!

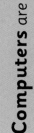

Technology is the use of science to make new and useful things.

Heart rate monitors tell us how fast our hearts beat.

Video games can be played on phones, tablets, computers, or game consoles.

My wheelchair is specially designed so I can go really fast!

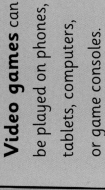

Wheelchairs are an amazing invention that help people move around and play sports, such as wheelchair basketball and rugby.

Plastic is a useful technology because it is a strong material. But it's also hard to get rid of because it never completely breaks down or goes away.

Before **phones** were invented, people living far apart wrote letters and had to wait days for a reply. Now, we can text or talk to each other straight away!

Money

People use money to **pay for things** that they need or want. This might be food, clothes, travel tickets, or toys. But before you can spend money, you have to earn it!

Making money

To earn money, people go to **work** and exchange their time and effort for money. There are many ways of paying for things, such as coins, notes, credit cards, cheques, and online payments.

Banks

Most people store their money in a bank account to keep it safe.

Before coins were invented, people used small objects such as beans and shells to buy and trade.

Cowry shell

Money of the world

If you travel to another country, the people there might use **different** money to what you're used to. In the UK they use pounds, in the USA they use dollars, in India they use rupees, and in South Africa they use rand. Which currency is used where you live?

Ancient Chinese coin →

Exchange rate

The money used in one country is usually worth a different amount to that of another. For example, 1 US dollar is worth roughly 120 Japanese yen, although this is always **changing**.

The first coins were used almost 3000 years ago!

What are things worth?

Different things are worth more or less than others. For example, a loaf of bread is worth a lot less than a car because it is easy to make, while a car uses expensive materials and takes a long time to make.

 =     =

Energy

Have you ever wondered why a light turns on when you flick a switch? It's because of **electricity** – a form of energy. We use energy to make all sorts of things happen.

Electricity is generated in power stations.

Types of energy

Energy comes in many different forms such as heat, sound, chemical, and mechanical. Just like a house needs electricity for power, your body needs the chemical energy you get from food.

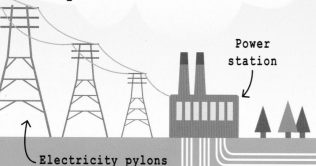

Power station

Electricity pylons

Electricity is carried through pylons and cables to buildings.

We need to generate a lot of electrical energy to power a

Wind turbines have huge blades that spin in the wind. This energy spins a generator, which turns it into electrical energy.

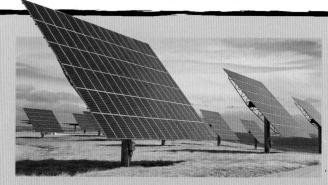

Solar panels collect light energy from the Sun to generate electricity. Some people generate electricity for their own home by having solar panels on their roof.

Solar panels

Kinetic (movement) energy allows things to move. It lets you run, jump, and dance!

Sound energy

Electrical energy turns into heat energy when a kettle boils.

The food we eat fuels our bodies.

Types of energy

Power sources such as coal and gas are known as **fossil fuels**. These sources are running out, and we can't make any more. However, energy from sunlight, wind, and water power are great ways to generate electricity, because they are renewable.

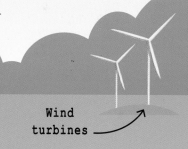

Wind turbines

whole city. Electricity is generated in a number of ways...

Water dams are built on rivers. Water is allowed to flow quickly through pipes, where it turns the blade of a turbine to generate electricity.

Coal, oil, and gas are the processed remains of plants and animals that died millions of years ago. Burning them releases energy, but it is very bad for the environment.

Getting around

There are hundreds of ways to get from place to place. How many of these types of **transport** have you tried?

Helicopter

Take to the **skies** and watch the busy world from **above**.

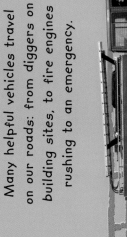

Tractor

Train

Fire engine

Many helpful vehicles travel on our roads: from diggers on building sites, to fire engines rushing to an emergency.

Aeroplane

Hot air balloon

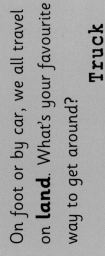

Truck

On foot or by car, we all travel on **land**. What's your favourite way to get around?

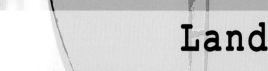

Sky

Land

Bicycle

Bus

Car

Motorbike

MAERSK

Container ship

Some ships are enormous and can transport large items like cars.

Yacht

GER 557

Lifeboat

Kayak

Cruise ship

Bobbing up and down in the **sea** can feel a bit strange, but it's a fun way to travel.

Sea

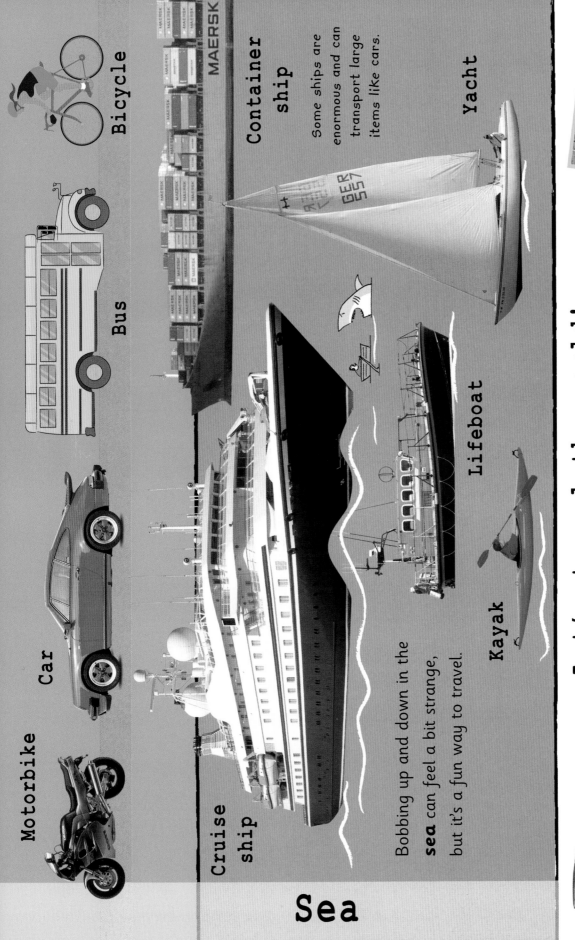

Let's travel the world!

Ride through a snowy forest on a sleigh pulled by huskies!

Hop on board a gondola and explore the busy canals in Venice, Italy.

Half motorcycle, half car, a tuk tuk is a fun way to travel around Thailand and India.

Incredible Internet

Satellite

Throughout the world, billions of computers **link together** to make the Internet. People from all over use the Internet to share information.

The World Wide Web is a collection of websites that exists on the Internet.

We can access the Internet on computers, smartphones, tablets, and more.

What can you do online?

Buy and sell things

Learn new things

Play games

Send messages

Download and stream pictures, music, and movies

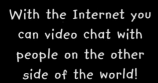

With the Internet you can video chat with people on the other side of the world!

How does it work?

Computers are linked together through cables, or wirelessly through satellites in space. Once they connect, computers can communicate to **exchange information** such as images, text, sound, and video.

We use programs called browsers to look at websites on the World Wide Web.

Taking care online

WARNING!

Before you use the Internet by yourself, look at the websites you use with a grown-up. They'll be able to tell you **which ones are safe**. If you see anything that upsets you, tell a grown-up straight away.

67

Social media

Social media is a great way to stay in touch with friends. But you need to **check with a parent** or carer before using it.

You can talk to people all OVER THE WORLD with social media.

Getting online

To use social media, you need a tablet, smartphone, or computer. If you don't have one at home, you might be able to use one at school or a library.

Staying safe

Remember these tips to keep you safe and happy on social media:

You have to be at least 13 years old to use most social media but there are special social media sites for children.

Keep your personal information very secret. Even photos of you in your school uniform could tell mean people how to find you in the real world.

Never talk to strangers online, even if they seem nice. You can never be sure of who they really are.

Don't forget to enjoy life offline!
Social media can make you care too much about what everyone thinks. You don't need to please others to be happy.

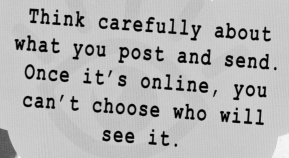

Think carefully about what you post and send. Once it's online, you can't choose who will see it.

Going on holiday

Travelling can be so much fun. People go on trips to relax, experience other cultures, and create new **memories** with their friends and family.

Types of holiday

People like to spend their time doing different things, so it's no surprise they like to go on different trips, too. Luckily, there's a holiday for everyone.

Some people like to live life on the edge. Instead of relaxing they prefer going on adventures such as mountain climbing, skydiving, scuba diving, or white water rafting.

Some people love to get back to nature. Going **camping** means they can sleep under the stars in the wilderness and toast marshmallows over a fire!

Whether it's by the beach or a hotel pool, a warm place with sunshine, sandcastles, and swimming is perfect for people looking to take in the scenery and relax.

There's nothing quite like the view from a mountain. That's one of the reasons people go **skiing**. Not to mention the thrill of zipping down mountains at rapid speeds!

Cruise ships are like massive floating hotels that sail from place to place. The huge ships have restaurants, pools, and activities to keep passengers happy.

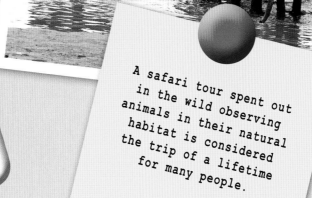

A safari tour spent out in the wild observing animals in their natural habitat is considered the trip of a lifetime for many people.

There are lots of amazing **cities** all over the world. Exploring them and taking in the exciting sights, sounds, food, and attractions is a wonderful experience.

71

At the beach

Do you prefer to laze in the sun, swim in the sea, or play in the sand? There's plenty to **do and see** at the beach!

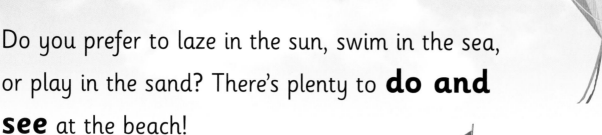

Some beaches have pebbles while others are covered in sand. Sand is made up of trillions of very tiny pieces of rock and minerals.

Beach volleyball

This beach game involves two teams hitting a ball over the net with their hands or arms. Don't let the ball touch the ground or hit the net!

Beach activities

Many people go to the beach to relax with a book, have a picnic, or sunbathe. Others enjoy swimming, surfing, collecting shells, building sandcastles, and playing games. What do you like to do?

The beach is fun, but it's important to stay safe. Don't swim unsupervised, and be sure to wear sunscreen.

Sailing

Sailors use the wind to move their boats around on the water. Take it at your own pace or take part in a race!

Snorkelling

Snorkellers wear a mask and breathe through a tube to look under the water without having to come up for air.

People and

culture

Have you ever wondered what life is like for **other people** around the planet? Do they go to a school like yours, eat the food you eat, or have the same interests? You may be surprised at how much you have in common with people all over the world.

Language

What do sharing knowledge, telling stories, and expressing emotions all have in common? They're all much, much **easier** thanks to language.

Hey!

How are you?

The 5 biggest languages

Chinese

Chinese is the most spoken language in the world with more than 1 billion speakers. There are different variations, but the most common is Mandarin.

Spanish

Spanish is the second most spoken language. It's spoken in countries all over the world.

People who speak more than one language are called "bilingual" or "multilingual".

English

English is spoken as a first language in more than 100 countries. It's also the world's most spoken second language.

Hola! (oh-lah)

Nǐhǎo! (nee-how)

Hello! (hell-low)

What is language?

Language is how people **communicate**. It can be spoken and written. People in different countries around the world use many different languages.

Bye!

Arabic

More than 200 million people across the Middle East and Africa speak varieties of Arabic.

Marhaban!
(mar-har-ban)

There are around 7,000 languages in the world.

Hindi

India has hundreds of languages, but the most common is Hindi. It has around 200 million speakers.

Namaste!
(nuh-muh-stay)

Other languages

Not all languages are spoken or written. People who are deaf can communicate using **sign language**, and blind people use a system called **Braille** to read.

Sign language

Braille

Even computer programs have their own languages!

World religions

Humans have always tried to figure out the **big questions** in life. Throughout the world, some people turn to religion to understand how to lead a good and meaningful life.

 Buddhism

 Christianity

 Sikhism

Followers: Buddhists
Place of worship: Vihara (temple)
Holy book: Tipitaka
Local leader: Lama

Buddhists follow the teachings of the Buddha, who lived more than 2,000 years ago.

Buddha

Followers: Christians
Place of worship: Church
Holy book: Bible
Local leader: Priest or minister

Church

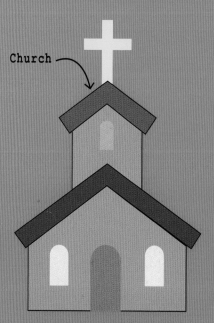

Christians believe that there is one God and that Jesus Christ is his son.

Followers: Sikhs
Place of worship: Gurdwara
Holy book: Sri Guru Granth Sahib, Dasam Granth
Local leader: None

Sikhs do not cut their hair as they believe keeping it naturally long helps to live in harmony with God.

I believe!

There are hundreds of religions, each with different beliefs. Some, but not all, worship or pray to a god or gods.

You don't have to believe in any god or religion.

The most important thing is to respect other people's way of life and beliefs.

 Judaism

 Islam

🕉 Hinduism

Followers: Jews
Place of worship: Synagogue
Holy book: Tanakh
Local leader: Rabbi

Chanukiah

Judaism is one of the oldest religions in the world. It has existed for around 3,500 years.

Followers: Muslims
Place of worship: Mosque
Holy book: Qur'an
Local leader: Imam

Muslims follow the five pillars of Islam. One of the pillars is Salat, praying to God, Allah, five times a day.

Prayer mat

Followers: Hindus
Place of worship: Mandir (temple)
Holy book: Vedas, Bhagavad Gita
Local leader: Pundit, guru

Hindus believe in many gods, including Brahma, Vishnu, Shiva, and Ganesh.

Shiva

79

Celebrations

All around the world, people love to celebrate! But some festivals are special to a place, culture, religion, or person.

Day of the Dead

In Mexico, people **remember** their ancestors on Día de los Muertos with gifts, food, and candles.

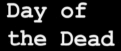

Birthdays

Throughout the world, we celebrate the day people are **born**, often with cake!

Weddings

Grown-ups get married when they want to **share their lives** together. Each culture has its own special wedding traditions.

Thanksgiving

During this harvest festival, family and friends share a **special dinner** and give thanks for what they have.

Hanukkah

This **Jewish Festival of Lights** lasts for eight days and celebrates the importance of hope.

Kwanzaa

This festival celebrates **African cultures** and communities with music, feasts, and special candles.

Why do we celebrate?

Whatever our traditions are, celebrations are often a time for loved ones to **come together**, remember what is important to them, and have fun!

New Year	Chinese New Year	Christmas
At midnight on December 31st, colourful fireworks fill the skies to mark the **start** of the New Year.	The New Year celebrations in China focus around **good fortune** for the coming year with families and friends. 	At Christmas, Christians remember the **birth of Jesus Christ** by going to church, decorating a tree, and sharing gifts. 
Mardi Gras	Carnival	Passover
On Mardi Gras, people have feasts and parade in **fancy dress**.	Carnival in Rio de Janeiro, Brazil, is a **huge festival**. It takes place every year before Lent.	Passover is a week-long Jewish festival to remember when **Moses** led the Jews to freedom. 

Let's **celebrate** some more!

Holi

Hindus celebrate love and the arrival of spring at this **festival of colours** by throwing colourful powder.

Diwali

For Diwali, the festival of lights, Hindus, Sikhs, and Jains light little candles called **diyas**.

Lantern Festival

On the last day of Chinese New Year, red lights are released in the sky.

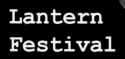

Ghost Festival

Hungry Ghost Festival is celebrated in many Asian countries in **memory** of those who have passed away.

Setsubun

Japan's Setsubun festival is held near the start of spring. One ritual involves people throwing soybeans as a way to **banish evil spirits**.

Yam Festival

Many West African cultures celebrate the **harvest** during the New Yam Festival.

Festival fun

Chasing cheese
Once a year, competitors in Gloucestershire, UK, chase a wheel of cheese as it rolls down a steep hill.

Food fight!
Buñol in Spain hosts an annual tomato-throwing festival, which is called La Tomatina. Tomato soup, anyone?

Glorious mud
At Mudfest in Boryeong, South Korea, thousands of people roll around in mud in one of the world's messiest festivals.

Ramadan

For a whole month, **Muslims** across the world do not eat or drink from sunrise to sunset.

Eid-al-Fitr

At the **end** of Ramadan, Muslims celebrate with a festival known as Eid-al-Fitr.

Eid feast

Baisakhi

Dancing, singing, and parades are part of Baisakhi, a **Sikh festival** to celebrate the new year.

Easter

Easter is a Christian celebration in spring based on the resurrection of **Jesus Christ**. Many countries celebrate by painting eggs.

Songkran

This Buddhist festival marks the start of the new year in Thailand with **water fights**!

Bodhi Day

On Bodhi Day, Buddhists remember how **Buddha** achieved enlightenment beneath the bodhi tree.

My clothes

Their main job is to keep us **warm**, but clothes can also have religious or cultural meaning. Some are functional but some are just fun!

My story

Our clothes can tell a story about us such as what we enjoy or maybe where we're from. What do your clothes say about you?

Thobe

Piupiu skirt

Hanbok

The hanbok is a traditional item of Korean clothing. It is worn on special occasions such as celebrations and festivals.

Beaded necklace

Beaded necklaces and clothing are worn by members of the Maasai tribe. Every bead means something.

Kilt

In parts of Scotland, it is traditional for men to wear knee length tartan skirts called kilts.

Fashion

Designers reveal new ideas for clothing at fashion shows. Fashion is **always changing** – its difficult to keep up with the latest trends!

Salwar kameez

A salwar kameez suit is traditionally worn in parts of India, Pakistan, and Bangladesh.

Clothes for when it's hot...

Shorts

Sunglasses

Sunhat

Swimsuit

Skirt

Flip-flops

Sundress

Clothes for when it's cold...

Hat

Coat

Trousers

Jumper

Mittens

Socks

Boots

Jeans

Scarf

Shopping

Need some new **clothes**? Or perhaps you want a shiny new **toy**? Time to go shopping!

Which shop?

There are lots of different types of shop, from furniture shops, to florists. Many shops sells particular items, for example a fishmonger only sells seafood.

Pharmacy

Not feeling well? Pharmacies sell medicines and other items to do with your health, as well as beauty products.

Clothes shop

As you grow, you will need bigger clothes. Head to the clothes shop to find new comfy clothes, a smart outfit, a coat, underwear, and pyjamas.

Supermarket

You can find a huge range of items at a supermarket! They sell food, cleaning products, cooking equipment, toys, clothes, books, and more.

Online shopping

Some people don't have time to visit the shops. They buy things online and get them delivered straight to their door. Online shops also offer lots of choice.

Hamleys, England
From teddy bears to go-karts, Hamleys sells just about every toy you can think of! It is one of the oldest toyshops in the world.

Marrakesh Souks, Morocco
One of the most exciting places to shop is in the souks of Marrakesh. You'll find rugs, clothing, spices, and lanterns.

Bookshop

Whether you like spooky stories, puzzles, or activity books, there will always be something exciting to buy and read at a bookshop.

Furniture shop

To make a house a home, you need some furniture! Furniture shops sell chairs, tables, sofas, beds, and cupboards.

Bangkok Floating Markets, Thailand
Ever seen a shop on water? Bangkok is famous for its floating markets, where traders sell tasty food from their boats.

Hobbies

How do you spend your time? Do you see friends, get lost in a book, go on adventures, or play games? Hobbies are the things we do for **fun**.

Nature

Do you like getting out and about? There's lots to do outdoors, such as fishing, camping, or bird watching.

Food

Explore cafés and restaurants to discover new, delicious dishes. Then you can try to cook them at home.

Arts

Do you like creating things? Drawing, photography, painting, and knitting are just a few fun and creative hobbies.

Films and TV

When you watch a movie or a TV show you can lose yourself in a story, learn something new, or just relax.

Computing

Time can pass in a flash when you're having fun playing computer games or learning things online.

Pets

Many people spend their time caring for pets. It can be time-consuming caring for an animal, but it's very rewarding!

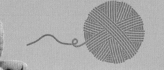

Many people take part in clubs or events in their community such as looking after a public garden. It's a great way to make friends and learn new things.

Music

If you love listening to music, you might also enjoy learning to play an instrument, or even singing.

Travel

Many people go on mini adventures in their local town or city, while others go abroad to experience places around the world.

Sports

Do you play basketball, dance, cycle, or do yoga? There are lots of active hobbies that will get you moving. It's also fun to watch and cheer on your favourite team!

Socializing

What do you do when you spend time with your friends? Do you play games, chat, or do something else?

Trips

Museums and galleries are filled with intriguing things to look at and learn about. Have you been to see a play, exhibition, or a music concert?

Reading

Turning the pages of a good book and escaping into a gripping story or learning fun facts is a great way to spend your time.

The world of art

Art comes in lots of forms, and means different things to different people – it's all a matter of **taste**!

Look at a piece of art up close, then look at it from further away. Does it seem different? Seeing something in a different way can change how you feel about it.

You can look at art collections in a GALLERY.

Painting

There are many types of paint and even more **styles** of painting. Some people paint with lots of detail, others make interesting shapes and patterns.

Murals

Art gives us clues about what life might have been like when it was made. The world's oldest paintings can be found on the **walls of caves**.

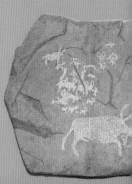

How do you feel?

Looking at art can make you feel different things. Bright colours can make you **happy** and cheer you up, while dull and dark colours might make you **feel sad** or upset.

Art can make us feel deep emotions or challenge the way we think.

Why not take a seat and think about what you see?

Photography

Photographers **capture their view** of the world with the click of a button!

Sculptures

Pieces of **3-D** art are called sculptures. They can be make from clay or stone, or carved into wood or other materials.

Playing games

Everyone loves to play games, and there are **so many** to choose from. Playing games can be a great way to exercise the body or mind, and make new friends.

Let's run!
Playing outside is lots of fun. From Tag and Hide and Seek, to Musical Statues, and Duck, Duck, Goose, there is something for everyone.

Corre, Corre la Guaraca is a game in Chile similar to Duck, Duck, Goose, but with an added handkerchief.

Do you know Rock, Paper, Scissors? What about the Sumatran version, Semut, Orang, Gajah (Ant, Man, Elephant)? Or perhaps Bird, Paper, Water from Malaysia?

Tinko, Tinko is a popular hand clapping game played in Nigeria.

The pieces on a chess board move in different ways.

Board games

There are thousands of board games, and some have been around for thousands of years! Chess was invented around 1,500 years ago in India.

Go board

Go was invented in China more than 2,500 years ago!

There are 52 cards in a standard deck.

Card games

A single pack of cards allows you to play hundreds of different games. From Snap and Old Maid, to Go Fish and Crazy Eights, cards are a great way to have fun on rainy days.

Sports

Whether played alone, with a friend, or on a team, there are hundreds of **sports** that are enjoyed by people all over the world. Are any of these your favourite?

Whee, we're skydiving!

Racing

For thrill-seekers who feel the need for speed, racing sports combine the power of man and machine. Drivers race around tracks at dizzying speeds!

Martial arts

Martial arts involve ways to defend yourself and beat an opponent in combat. There are lots of types, including karate, wrestling, and judo.

Archery

Bullseye! For years archers used a bow and arrows to fight or hunt, but it is now a sport. Archers need a keen eye and steady hand.

Football

Football involves a team of players trying to kick a ball into the other team's goal. But you probably knew that – it's the most popular sport in the world!

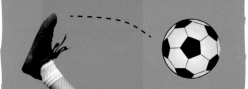

Cricket

Cricket is another of the world's most popular sports. Each team hits a hard ball with a bat and tries to score more runs than the other team.

Does anyone know where I can plug this in?

Unusual sports

Some of the most interesting sports are the most unusual. Extreme ironing, toe wrestling, and cheese rolling are all great examples!

Athletics

Run, jump, throw, and more. Athletics is all about being the fastest, strongest, or most skilled. It's the biggest part of the Olympic games.

Skiing

Skiing combines speed, skill, and snow – perfect for daredevils who want to zip down mountains at rapid speeds. Warm clothes and nerves of steel are a must!

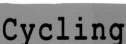

Sailing

Whether it's for pleasure or as part of a race, sailing uses the power of the wind to move boats through the water. Watch out for waves!

Tennis

Tennis players use their power and skill to hit a ball over a net. That may sound simple, but it isn't when an opponent is hitting it back!

Cycling

From high-flying BMX stunts or mountain bikes speeding down tracks, to gruelling races like the Tour de France, cycling is a sport with many forms.

Gymnastics

Gymnasts move in ways that seem impossible. Balance beam, rings, pommel horse, and trampolining are all gymnastics events.

Golf

Golf is sometimes called the sport where you are your own opponent. The aim is to strike a ball with a club and get it into a hole.

Sporting events

Playing sport is lots of fun, but it's also fun to watch the strongest, fastest, and most skillful athletes compete against each other at the **highest level**.

The World Cup

Football's biggest tournament is the World Cup. Countries from around the world face off every **four years** to see who is best. It's watched by billions of people.

The Opens

The biggest tennis tournaments in the world are Wimbledon, the US Open, French Open, and Australian Open.

The first modern Olympic games took place in

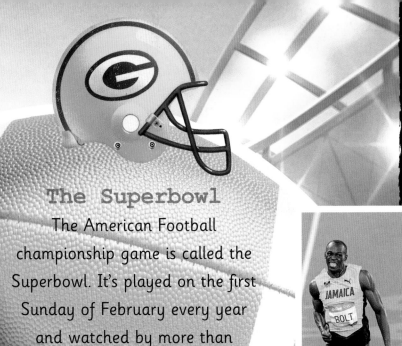

The Superbowl

The American Football championship game is called the Superbowl. It's played on the first Sunday of February every year and watched by more than 100 million Americans.

The Olympics

Every four years, the best athletes from almost all the world's countries compete against each other in athletics, cycling, swimming, and more, to win **medals** and glory for their countries.

World Drivers' Championship

Formula One takes place over a season on courses all over the world. The drivers with the most points at the end of the season wins.

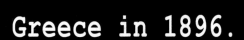

Greece in 1896.

Libraries

When you think of a library, you probably think of **books**, but libraries provide other services to help and entertain people.

The largest library in the world is the Library of Congress in Washington, USA. It holds over 39 million books and other printed materials – that's a lot of reading!

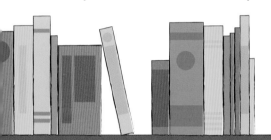 

As well as public ones, libraries can be found in

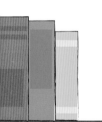     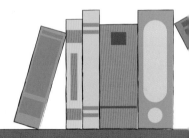

A world of books

From exciting stories, to tales of the past, books teach us about the world and provide us with hours of entertainment, too!

 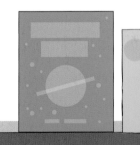

Using a library

Libraries are amazing places that let you **borrow books** for a little while. Visit your local library and find something fun or interesting. If you run out of time before finishing, you can always renew them.

I choose books for my library and **ORGANIZE** them so people can find what they need.

SCHOOLS, HOSPITALS, and PRISONS.

Many large libraries have more than just books. They have computers, films, music, audiobooks, puzzles, and more. In some areas of the world you can even borrow art to take home and hang on your wall!

Librarian

Museums

Filled with interesting objects from around the world, museums teach us about **history**, **science**, **art**, **culture**, and just about any topic you can think of!

The Mona Lisa is a famous painting that hangs in the Louvre, France.

For everyone

Museums are open to everyone and many are **free**. The first public museum was built in 1683 in Oxford, England. There are now more than 55,000 museums around the world.

People who organize museum collections are called curators.

There are some WEIRD and WACKY museums around the world.

In Mexico, people can snorkel to an **Underwater** museum with nearly 500 sculptures on the ocean floor.

There is even a **museum of toilets** in India, which has a golden toilet on display!

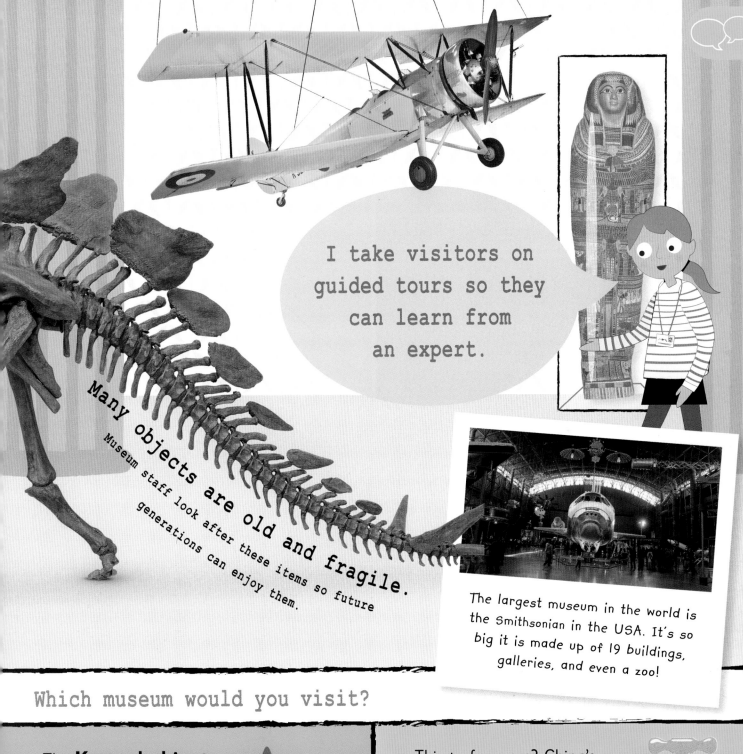

I take visitors on guided tours so they can learn from an expert.

Many objects are old and fragile. Museum staff look after these items so future generations can enjoy them.

The largest museum in the world is the Smithsonian in the USA. It's so big it is made up of 19 buildings, galleries, and even a zoo!

Which museum would you visit?

The **Kattenkabinet ("Cat Cabinet") Museum** in the Netherlands is filled with all things cat-related.

Thirsty for more? China's **Museum of Tap Water** is quite literally a fountain of knowledge!

The **big wide** world

Our planet is **huge**, which means there is lots to learn about it and there's always somewhere to explore! Do you know your North Pole from your South Pole, or your countries from your continents? Well, read on and you soon will!

It takes a long time to travel around the Earth!

A long, long time ago all the continents were joined together into one big supercontinent called Pangaea.

North America

Continents

Planet Earth is mostly water, but all the land is split into seven big chunks called **continents**. These continents are also split into smaller chunks called countries.

South America

Do you know which continent you live on? I bet it's not Antarctica!

From round to flat

Because the **Earth is round**, it's impossible to make a perfect flat map of it — something will always get distorted. There are different versions of maps with different distortions. We call these different maps **projections**.

Europe

Asia is the biggest continent.

Asia

Many countries in the Pacific islands aren't part of any continent.

Africa

Australia

Antarctica is very cold. Scientists go there to work, but nobody lives there all the time.

Gerardus Mercator

Antarctica

The most common map projection is the **Mercator projection**. Directions and distances look quite accurate, but places far away from the middle of the Earth look bigger than they really are.

Greenland

Africa

Distortion in the Mercator projection makes the country Greenland look bigger than Africa. In reality it's 14 times smaller!

The equator

If the North Pole is at the top of the Earth and the South Pole is at the bottom, **what's in the middle?** It's an imaginary line around the centre of the Earth called the equator.

"Middle of the World Monument" in Ecuador, has a physical equator line.

Splitting the world

The equator divides the Earth into two halves. Anything above the equator is part of the **Northern Hemisphere**, and anything below is part of the **Southern Hemisphere**.

North Pole

Northern Hemisphere

Southern Hemisphere

If it were possible to walk around the equator, it would take about 20 million steps!

Places near the equator are hotter because the Sun's rays hit them at a more direct angle.

Places on Earth are in different **climate** (weather) zones based on how close or far away they are from the equator.

Polar

Temperate

Subtropical

Tropical

The equator

Tropical

Subtropical

Temperate

Polar

South Pole

Tropical zones

These places are hot and damp most of the year. They can be very stormy.

Subtropical zones

These places have long, hot, dry summers and wet, short winters.

Temperate zones

Places in temperate zones mostly have warm summers and cold winters.

Polar zones

The polar regions are very cold and dry. Winters are long and dark and summers are sunny but still very cold.

People who live in the Northern Hemisphere will see different stars than people who live in the Southern Hemisphere.

North America

With its frozen mountains, vast grasslands, tropics, and vibrant cities filled with people, the continent of North America is incredibly **diverse**.

North America has 23 countries. Many of them are islands.

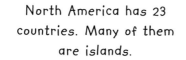

The Grand Canyon is a huge canyon in the USA. It's a very popular tourist spot.

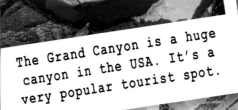

Chichén Itzá is a city of ruins in Mexico that was built thousands of years ago.

The bottom of North America is known as Central America.

Northern Canada is one of the best places to see the spectacular northern lights.

New York City is the biggest and most populated city in the USA.

The largest country in North America is Canada.

The beaches of the Caribbean Islands are some of the most beautiful on Earth.

Countries in North America

Antigua and Barbuda

Bahamas

Barbados

Belize

Canada

Costa Rica

Cuba

Dominica

Dominican Republic

El Salvador

Grenada

Guatemala

Haiti

Honduras

Jamaica

Mexico

Nicaragua

Panama

Saint Kitts and Nevis

Saint Lucia

Saint Vincent and the Grenadines

Trinidad and Tobago

United States of America

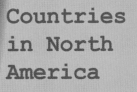

South America

This beautiful continent is home to **vibrant cultures**, lush rainforests, winding rivers, and much more.

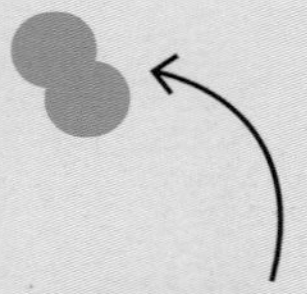

2

An enormous statue of Jesus Christ looks over Rio de Janeiro, Brazil.

1

Angel Falls in Venezuela is the world's tallest waterfall.

The Galápagos Islands are home to many unique animals, such as the marine iguana.

Galápagos Islands

3

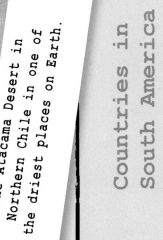

The Atacama Desert in Northern Chile in one of the driest places on Earth.

2

3

Countries in South America

Argentina

Bolivia

Brazil

Chile

Colombia

Ecuador

Guyana

Paraguay

Peru

Suriname

Uruguay

Venezuela

4

4

This frozen glacier is found near the tip of South America in Patagonia, Argentina.

Europe

Although it is the second smallest continent in size,
Europe is the third most populated continent.
It has a **rich history** and diverse culture.

Europe attracts
more than half a billion
tourists every year.

The old city of Venice, Italy is built on islands. People get around canals on boats.

2

3

1

1

4

Europe covers only 2 per cent of the Earth's surface.

2

The world's first ice hotel is in Sweden – even the beds are made of ice!

3

The largest art museum in the world is the Louvre in Paris, France.

Vatican City is the smallest country in the world.

4

There are over 6000 Greek islands and islets.

Countries in Europe

Albania	Latvia
Andorra	Liechtenstein
Austria	Lithuania
Belarus	Luxembourg
Belgium	Malta
Bosnia and	Moldova
Herzegovina	Monaco
Bulgaria	Montenegro
Croatia	Netherlands
Cyprus	North Macedonia
Czech Republic	Norway
Denmark	Poland
Estonia	Portugal
Finland	Romania
France	San Marino
Germany	Serbia
Greece	Slovakia
Holy See	Slovenia
(Vatican City)	Spain
Hungary	Sweden
Iceland	Switzerland
Ireland	Ukraine
Italy	United Kingdom
Kosovo (disputed)	

Asia

Asia is a huge mix of landscapes, people, and cultures. Not only is it the **biggest** continent, it's also the most populated.

Arashiyama is a huge forest of bamboo trees in Kyoto, Japan.

The Golden Temple in India is one of the most visited places in the whole world.

Mount Everest, the highest point on Earth, is located in Nepal.

Angkor Wat in Cambodia is the largest religious monument in the world.

Asia is one of the most diverse continents, and there's a huge mix of the old and the new.

4

Huge rice fields can be found in countries such as Vietnam, Thailand, and Bangladesh.

1

More than half of all the people in the world live in Asia!

Countries in Asia

Afghanistan	Maldives
Armenia	Mongolia
Azerbaijan*	Myanmar
Bahrain	Nepal
Bangladesh	North Korea
Bhutan	Oman
Brunei	Pakistan
Cambodia	Philippines
China	Qatar
East Timor	Russia*
Georgia*	Saudi Arabia
India	Singapore
Indonesia	South Korea
Iran	Sri Lanka
Iraq	Syria
Israel	Taiwan (Disputed)
Japan	Tajikistan
Jordan	Thailand
Kazakhstan*	Turkey*
Kuwait	Turkmenistan
Kyrgyzstan	United Arab Emirates
Laos	Uzbekistan
Lebanon	Vietnam
Malaysia	Yemen

* These countries have borders in both Europe and Asia, but are generally counted as part of Asia.

Oceania

The continent of Australia and countries such as New Zealand and Fiji, which **aren't part of any** continent, make up the region of Oceania.

1

One of the most famous buildings in Australia is the beautiful Sydney Opera House.

3

3

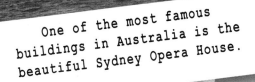

Australia's Lake Hillier is very salty and pink.

Australia is both a continent AND a country!

There are more than 10,000 total islands in Oceania!

Vanuatu is home to Mount Yasur - one of the most active volcanoes on Earth.

Countries in Oceania

Australia
Fiji
Kiribati
Marshall Islands
Micronesia
Nauru
New Zealand
Palau
Papua New Guinea
Samoa
Solomon Islands
Tonga
Tuvalu
Vanuatu

The country of Fiji is made up of more than 300 different islands.

Franz Josef Glacier in New Zealand is a popular spot for adventurers.

People from New Zealand are known as "Kiwis", after New Zealand's flightless kiwi bird.

The Poles

The **North** and **South Pole** are found at opposite sides of the Earth.

The North Pole is at the top, and the South Pole is at the bottom.

The North Pole

The North Pole is in the **Arctic.** There is no land there but the sea is frozen solid. The ice grows and shrinks with the seasons.

Russia

ARCTIC

NORTH POLE

Canada

Greenland

Polar bears live in the Arctic. Our fur and layers of fat keep us warm.

Native people have adapted to life in the Arctic.

The South Pole

The South Pole is in **Antarctica**, which is land covered in ice and surrounded by freezing sea. Antarctica is the coldest, driest, windiest place on Earth.

North Pole

South Pole

There are no towns in Antarctica, but scientists travel there to work in special research stations.

McMurdo Station

The largest base in Antarctica is McMurdo Station. More than 1,000 people can stay there at a time.

ANTARCTICA

SOUTH POLE

McMurdo Station

Southern Ocean

King penguins are among the only animals that can survive the Antarctic cold.

It almost NEVER RAINS in Antarctica. It is a cold desert.

Islands

An island is an area of land that is completely **surrounded by water**. Islands can be tiny or absolutely huge.

Indonesia is made up of around 17,000 islands.

It takes a very long time for islands to form.

There are **MANY TYPES** of island, but the

Continental islands start off as part of a continent but either break away, or are cut off when the sea level rises.

Soft rock gradually wears away, forming a trench.

Soft rock

The trench floods.

An island forms.

The world's largest island is Greenland. It's so big, the three next largest islands (New Guinea, Borneo, and Madagascar) could all fit inside it.

A group of islands close together is called an archipelago.

Archipelago

Madagascar is the fourth largest island in the world. Most of the plants and animals found there don't exist anywhere else on Earth.

There are more than 100,000 islands on Earth!

main types are continental and oceanic.

Oceanic islands are formed when underwater volcanoes erupt. The Hawaiian Islands are oceanic islands.

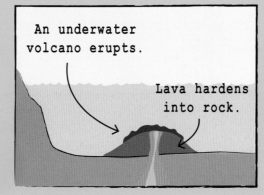

An underwater volcano erupts.

Lava hardens into rock.

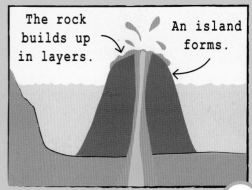

The rock builds up in layers.

An island forms.

Populations

There are around 7.5 billion people on Earth, although we can never be sure of the exact number as it's **always changing**. Here's where they all live.

North America

COUNTRY	POPULATION
United States	329,256,465
Mexico	125,959,205
Canada	35,881,659
Guatemala	16,581,273
Cuba	11,116,396
Haiti	10,788,440
Dominican Republic	10,298,756
Honduras	9,182,766
El Salvador	6,187,271
Nicaragua	6,085,213
Costa Rica	4,987,142
Panama	3,800,644
Jamaica	2,812,090
Trinidad and Tobago	1,215,527
Belize	385,854
Bahamas	332,634
Barbados	293,131
Saint Lucia	165,510
Grenada	112,207
Saint Vincent and Grenadines	101,844
Antigua and Barbuda	95,882
Dominica	74,027
Saint Kitts and Nevis	53,094

Africa

COUNTRY	POPULATION	COUNTRY	POPULATION
Nigeria	203,452,505	Burundi	11,844,520
Ethiopia	108,386,391	Tunisia	11,516,189
Egypt	99,413,317	Benin	11,340,504
Congo, Democratic Republic of The	85,281,024	Somalia	11,259,029
		South Sudan	10,204,581
Tanzania	55,451,343	Togo	8,176,449
South Africa	55,380,210	Libya	6,754,507
Kenya	48,397,527	Sierra Leone	6,312,212
Sudan	43,120,843	Eritrea	5,970,646
Algeria	41,657,488	Central African Republic	5,745,062
Uganda	40,853,749	Congo, Republic of The	5,062,021
Morocco	34,314,130	Liberia	4,809,768
Angola	30,355,880	Mauritania	3,840,429
Ghana	28,102,471	Namibia	2,533,224
Mozambique	27,233,789	Botswana	2,249,104
Côte d'Ivoire	26,260,582	Gabon	2,119,036
Madagascar	25,683,610	Gambia	2,092,731
Cameroon	25,640,965	Lesotho	1,962,461
Niger	19,866,231	Guinea-Bissau	1,833,247
Malawi	19,842,560	Mauritius	1,364,283
Burkina Faso	19,742,715	Eswatini	1,087,200
Mali	18,429,893	Djibouti	884,017
Zambia	16,445,079	Comoros	821,164
Chad	15,833,116	Equatorial Guinea	797,457
Senegal	15,020,945	Cape Verde	568,373
Zimbabwe	14,030,368	São Tomé and Príncipe	204,454
Rwanda	12,187,400	Seychelles	94,633
Guinea	11,855,411		

These numbers show how many people live in each country. Find yours!

Azerbaijan, Georgia, Kazakhstan, Russia, and Turkey have borders in both Europe and Asia.

Europe

COUNTRY	POPULATION
Germany	80,457,737
France	67,364,357
United Kingdom	65,105,246
Italy	62,246,674
Spain	49,331,076
Ukraine	43,952,299
Poland	38,420,687
Romania	21,457,116
Netherlands	17,151,228
Belgium	11,570,762
Greece	10,761,523
Czech Republic	10,686,269
Portugal	10,355,493
Sweden	10,040,995
Hungary	9,825,704
Belarus	9,527,543
Austria	8,793,370
Switzerland	8,292,809
Serbia	7,078,110
Bulgaria	7,057,504
Denmark	5,809,502
Finland	5,537,364
Slovakia	5,445,040
Norway	5,372,191
Ireland	5,068,050
Croatia	4,270,480
Bosnia and Herzegovina	3,849,891
Moldova	3,437,720
Albania	3,057,220
Lithuania	2,793,284
North Macedonia	2,118,945
Slovenia	2,102,126
Latvia	1,923,559
Kosovo (Disputed)	1,907,592
Estonia	1,244,288
Cyprus	1,237,088
Montenegro	614,249
Luxembourg	605,764
Malta	449,043
Iceland	343,518
Andorra	85,708
Liechtenstein	38,547
San Marino	33,779
Monaco	30,727
Holy See (Vatican City)	1,000

Asia

COUNTRY	POPULATION	COUNTRY	POPULATION
China	1,384,688,986	Kazakhstan	18,744,548
India	1,296,834,042	Cambodia	16,449,519
Indonesia	262,787,403	Jordan	10,458,413
Pakistan	207,862,518	Azerbaijan	10,046,516
Bangladesh	159,453,001	United Arab Emirates	9,701,315
Russia	142,122,776	Tajikistan	8,604,882
Japan	126,168,156	Israel	8,424,904
Philippines	105,893,381	Laos	7,234,171
Vietnam	97,040,334	Lebanon	6,100,075
Iran	83,024,745	Singapore	5,995,991
Turkey	81,257,239	Kyrgyzstan	5,849,296
Thailand	68,615,858	Turkmenistan	5,411,012
Myanmar	55,622,506	Georgia	4,926,087
South Korea	51,418,097	Oman	3,494,116
Iraq	40,194,216	Mongolia	3,103,428
Afghanistan	34,940,837	Armenia	3,038,217
Saudi Arabia	33,091,113	Kuwait	2,916,467
Malaysia	31,809,660	Qatar	2,363,569
Uzbekistan	30,023,709	Bahrain	1,442,659
Nepal	29,717,587	East Timor	1,321,929
Yemen	28,667,230	Bhutan	766,397
North Korea	25,381,085	Brunei	450,565
Taiwan (Disputed)	23,545,963	Maldives	392,473
Sri Lanka	22,576,592		
Syria	19,454,263		

Oceania

COUNTRY	POPULATION
Australia	23,470,145
Papua New Guinea	7,027,332
New Zealand	4,545,627
Fiji	926,276
Solomon Islands	660,121
Vanuatu	288,037
Samoa	201,316
Kiribati	109,367
Tonga	106,398
Federated States of Micronesia	103,643
Marshall Islands	75,684
Palau	21,516
Tuvalu	11,147
Nauru	9,692

South America

COUNTRY	POPULATION
Brazil	208,846,892
Colombia	48,168,996
Argentina	44,694,198
Venezuela	31,689,176
Peru	31,331,228
Chile	17,925,262
Ecuador	16,498,502
Bolivia	11,306,341
Paraguay	7,025,763
Uruguay	3,369,299
Guyana	740,685
Suriname	597,927

125

Country size

Some countries are very big and others are tiny. Is your country big, small, or something **inbetween**?

North America

COUNTRY	SIZE
Canada	9,984,670
United States	9,833,517
Mexico	1,964,375
Nicaragua	130,370
Honduras	112,090
Cuba	110,860
Guatemala	108,889
Panama	75,420
Costa Rica	51,100
Dominican Republic	48,670
Haiti	27,750
Belize	22,966
El Salvador	21,041
Bahamas	13,880
Jamaica	10,991
Trinidad and Tobago	5,128
Dominica	751
Saint Lucia	616
Antigua and Barbuda	443
Barbados	430
Saint Vincent and Grenadines	389
Grenada	344
Saint Kitts and Nevis	261

Africa

COUNTRY	SIZE	COUNTRY	SIZE
Algeria	2,381,741	Côte d'Ivoire	322,463
Congo, Democratic Republic of The	2,344,858	Burkina Faso	274,200
		Gabon	267,667
Sudan	1,861,484	Guinea	245,857
Libya	1,759,540	Uganda	241,038
Chad	1,284,000	Ghana	238,533
Niger	1,267,000	Senegal	196,722
Angola	1,246,700	Tunisia	163,610
Mali	1,240,192	Malawi	118,484
South Africa	1,219,090	Eritrea	117,600
Ethiopia	1,104,300	Benin	112,622
Mauritania	1,030,700	Liberia	111,369
Egypt	1,001,450	Sierra Leone	71,740
Tanzania	947,300	Togo	56,785
Nigeria	923,768	Guinea-Bissau	36,125
Namibia	824,292	Lesotho	30,355
Mozambique	799,380	Equatorial Guinea	28,051
Zambia	752,618	Burundi	27,830
South Sudan	644,329	Rwanda	26,338
Somalia	637,657	Djibouti	23,200
Central African Republic	622,984	Eswatini	17,364
Madagascar	587,041	Gambia	11,300
Botswana	581,730	Cape Verde	4,033
Kenya	580,367	Comoros	2,235
Cameroon	475,440	Mauritius	2,040
Morocco	446,550	São Tomé and Príncipe	964
Zimbabwe	390,757	Seychelles	455
Congo, Republic of The	342,000		

South America

COUNTRY	SIZE
Brazil	8,515,770
Argentina	2,780,400
Peru	1,285,216
Colombia	1,138,910
Bolivia	1,098,581
Venezuela	912,050
Chile	756,102
Paraguay	406,752
Ecuador	283,561
Guyana	214,969
Uruguay	176,215
Suriname	163,820

These measurements are all in "Square Kilometres".

Europe

COUNTRY	SIZE
France	643,801
Ukraine	603,550
Spain	505,370
Sweden	450,295
Germany	357,022
Finland	338,145
Norway	323,802
Poland	312,685
Italy	301,340
United Kingdom	243,610
Romania	238,391
Belarus	207,600
Greece	131,957
Bulgaria	110,879
Iceland	103,000
Hungary	93,028
Portugal	92,090
Austria	83,871
Czech Republic	78,867
Serbia	77,474
Ireland	70,273
Lithuania	65,300
Latvia	64,589
Croatia	56,594
Bosnia and Herzegovina	51,197
Slovakia	49,035
Estonia	45,228
Denmark	43,094
Netherlands	41,543
Switzerland	41,277
Moldova	33,851
Belgium	30,528
Albania	28,748
North Macedonia	25,713
Slovenia	20,273
Montenegro	13,812
Kosovo (Disputed)	10,887
Cyprus	9,251
Luxembourg	2,586
Andorra	468
Malta	316
Liechtenstein	160
San Marino	61
Monaco	2
Holy See (Vatican City)	0

Asia

COUNTRY	SIZE	COUNTRY	SIZE
Russia	17,098,242	Syria	185,180
China	9,596,960	Cambodia	181,035
India	3,287,263	Bangladesh	148,460
Kazakhstan	2,724,900	Nepal	147,181
Saudi Arabia	2,149,690	Tajikistan	144,100
Indonesia	1,904,569	North Korea	120,538
Iran	1,648,195	South Korea	99,720
Mongolia	1,564,116	Jordan	89,342
Pakistan	796,095	Azerbaijan	86,600
Turkey	783,562	United Arab Emirates	83,600
Myanmar	676,578	Georgia	69,700
Afghanistan	652,230	Sri Lanka	65,610
Yemen	527,968	Bhutan	38,394
Thailand	513,120	Taiwan (Disputed)	35,980
Turkmenistan	488,100	Armenia	29,743
Uzbekistan	447,400	Israel	20,770
Iraq	438,317	Kuwait	17,818
Japan	377,915	East Timor	14,874
Vietnam	331,210	Qatar	11,586
Malaysia	329,847	Lebanon	10,400
Oman	309,500	Brunei	5,765
Philippines	300,000	Bahrain	760
Laos	236,800	Singapore	697
Kyrgyzstan	199,951	Maldives	298

Oceania

COUNTRY	SIZE
Australia	7,741,220
Papua New Guinea	462,840
New Zealand	268,838
Solomon Islands	28,896
Fiji	18,274
Vanuatu	12,189
Samoa	2,831
Kiribati	811
Tonga	747
Federated States of Micronesia	702
Palau	459
Marshall Islands	181
Tuvalu	26
Nauru	21

Russia is by far the biggest country in the world. It shares a border with 14 other countries, and is almost the size of Pluto!

Capitals

Nearly every country has a **capital city**. This is usually the city where the country's government is based.

Nauru doesn't have a capital, but its government is based in a city called Yaren.

NORTH AMERICA

Antigua and Barbuda St. John's
Bahamas Nassau
Barbados Bridgetown
Belize Belmopan
Canada Ottawa
Costa Rica San José
Cuba Havana
Dominica Roseau
Dominican Republic Santo Domingo
El Salvador San Salvador
Grenada St. George's
Guatemala Guatemala City
Haiti Port-au-Prince
Honduras Tegucigalpa
Jamaica Kingston
Mexico Mexico City
Nicaragua Managua
Panama Panama City
Saint Kitts and Nevis Basseterre
Saint Lucia Castries
Saint Vincent and the Grenadines Kingstown

Trinidad and Tobago Port of Spain
United States Washington D.C.

SOUTH AMERICA

Argentina Buenos Aires
Bolivia Sucre
Brazil Brasilia
Chile Santiago
Colombia Bogotá
Ecuador Quito
Guyana Georgetown
Paraguay Asunción
Peru Lima
Suriname Paramaribo
Uruguay Montevideo
Venezuela Caracas

AFRICA

Algeria Algiers
Angola Luanda
Benin Porto-Novo
Botswana Gaborone
Burkina Faso Ouagadougou
Burundi Gitega
Cameroon Yaoundé
Cape Verde Praia
Central African Republic Bangui
Chad N'Djamena
Comoros Moroni
Congo, Democratic Republic of The Kinshasa
Congo, Republic of The Brazzaville
Côte d'Ivoire Yamoussoukro
Djibouti Djibouti
Egypt Cairo
Equatorial Guinea Malabo
Eritrea Asmara
Eswatini Mbabane
Ethiopia Addis Ababa
Gabon Libreville
Gambia Banjul
Ghana Accra
Guinea Conakry
Guinea-Bissau Bissau
Kenya Nairobi
Lesotho Maseru
Liberia Monrovia
Libya Tripoli
Madagascar Antananarivo
Malawi Lilongwe
Mali Bamako
Mauritania Nouakchott
Mauritius Port Louis
Morocco Rabat
Mozambique Maputo
Namibia Windhoek
Niger Niamey
Nigeria Abuja

Rwanda Kigali
São Tomé and Príncipe
São Tomé
Senegal Dakar
Seychelles Victoria
Sierra Leone Freetown
Somalia Mogadishu
South Africa Pretoria
South Sudan Juba
Sudan Khartoum
Tanzania Dodoma
Togo Lomé
Tunisia Tunis
Uganda Kampala
Zambia Lusaka
Zimbabwe Harare

ASIA

Afghanistan Kabul
Armenia Yerevan
Azerbaijan Baku
Bahrain Manama
Bangladesh Dhaka
Bhutan Thimphu
Brunei Bandar
Seri Begawan
Cambodia Phnom Penh
China Beijing
East Timor Dili
Georgia Tbilisi
India New Delhi
Indonesia Jakarta
Iran Tehran
Iraq Baghdad

Israel Jerusalem
Japan Tokyo
Jordan Amman
Kazakhstan Astana
Kuwait Kuwait City
Kyrgyzstan Bishkek
Laos Vientiane
Lebanon Beirut
Malaysia Kuala Lumpur
Maldives Malé
Mongolia Ulaanbaatar
Myanmar Naypyidaw
Nepal Kathmandu
North Korea Pyongyang
Oman Muscat
Pakistan Islamabad
Philippines Manila
Qatar Doha

Russia Moscow
Saudi Arabia Riyadh
Singapore Singapore
South Korea Seoul
Sri Lanka Colombo
Syria Damascus
Taiwan (Disputed)
Taipei
Tajikistan Dushanbe
Thailand Bangkok
Turkey Ankara
Turkmenistan Ashgabat
United Arab Emirates
Abu Dhabi
Uzbekistan Tashkent
Vietnam Hanoi
Yemen Sana'a

EUROPE

Albania Tirana
Andorra Andorra la Vella
Austria Vienna
Belarus Minsk
Belgium Brussels
Bosnia and Herzegovina
Sarajevo
Bulgaria Sofia
Croatia Zagreb
Cyprus Nicosia
Czech Republic Prague
Denmark Copenhagen
Estonia Tallinn
Finland Helsinki
France Paris
Germany Berlin
Greece Athens
Holy See Vatican City
Hungary Budapest
Iceland Reykjavík
Ireland Dublin
Italy Rome
Kosovo (Disputed) Pristina

Latvia Riga
Liechtenstein Vaduz
Lithuania Vilnius
Luxembourg Luxembourg
Malta Valletta
Moldova Chisinau
Monaco Monaco
Montenegro Podgorica
Netherlands Amsterdam
North Macedonia Skopje
Norway Oslo
Poland Warsaw
Portugal Lisbon
Romania Bucharest
San Marino San Marino
Serbia Belgrade
Slovakia Bratislava
Slovenia Ljubljana
Spain Madrid
Sweden Stockholm
Switzerland Bern
Ukraine Kiev
United Kingdom London

OCEANIA

Australia Canberra
Federated States
of Micronesia Palikir
Fiji Suva
Kiribati Tarawa
Marshall Islands
Majuro
Nauru (No Capital)
New Zealand
Wellington
Palau Ngerulmud
Papua New
Guinea Port Moresby
Samoa Apia
Solomon Islands
Honiara
Tonga Nuku'alofa
Tuvalu Funafuti
Vanuatu Port Vila

Flags

Each country has a flag that it uses as a **symbol of its nation**. Do you see yours?

North America

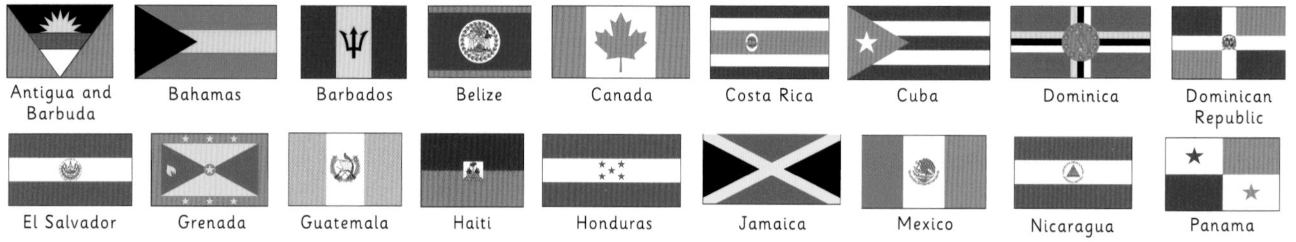

Antigua and Barbuda, Bahamas, Barbados, Belize, Canada, Costa Rica, Cuba, Dominica, Dominican Republic, El Salvador, Grenada, Guatemala, Haiti, Honduras, Jamaica, Mexico, Nicaragua, Panama, Saint Kitts and Nevis, Saint Lucia, Saint Vincent and the Grenadines, Trinidad and Tobago, United States

South America

Argentina, Bolivia, Brazil, Chile, Colombia, Ecuador, Guyana, Paraguay, Peru, Suriname, Uruguay, Venezuela

Africa

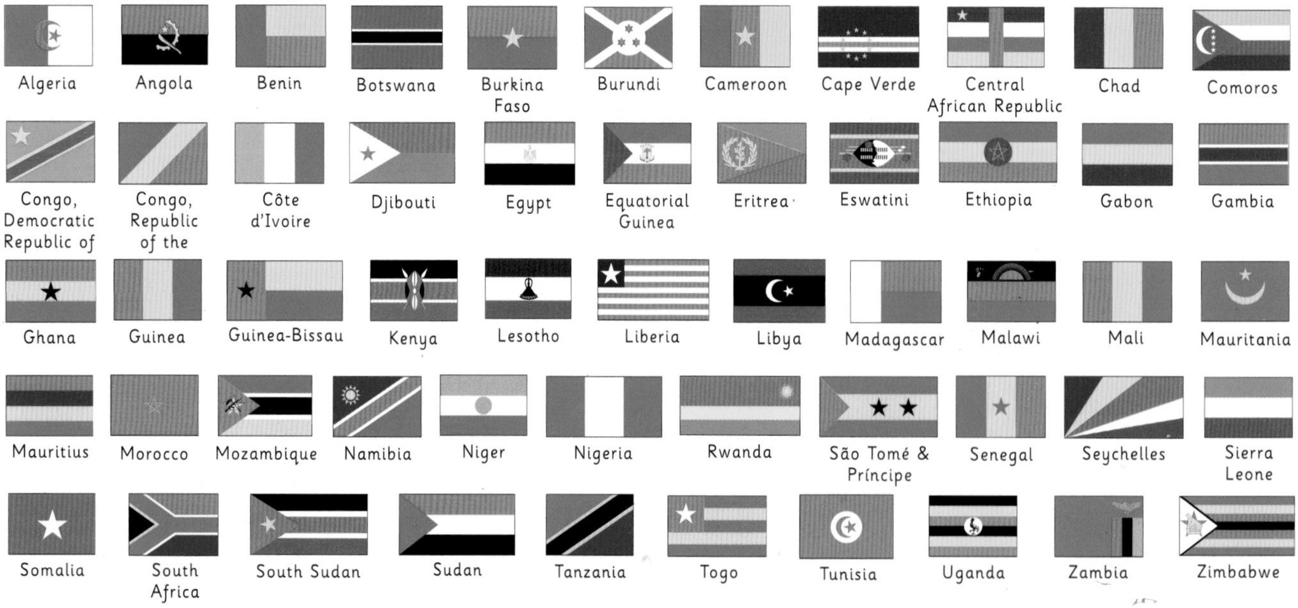

Algeria, Angola, Benin, Botswana, Burkina Faso, Burundi, Cameroon, Cape Verde, Central African Republic, Chad, Comoros, Congo, Democratic Republic of, Congo, Republic of the, Côte d'Ivoire, Djibouti, Egypt, Equatorial Guinea, Eritrea, Eswatini, Ethiopia, Gabon, Gambia, Ghana, Guinea, Guinea-Bissau, Kenya, Lesotho, Liberia, Libya, Madagascar, Malawi, Mali, Mauritania, Mauritius, Morocco, Mozambique, Namibia, Niger, Nigeria, Rwanda, São Tomé & Príncipe, Senegal, Seychelles, Sierra Leone, Somalia, South Africa, South Sudan, Sudan, Tanzania, Togo, Tunisia, Uganda, Zambia, Zimbabwe

Europe

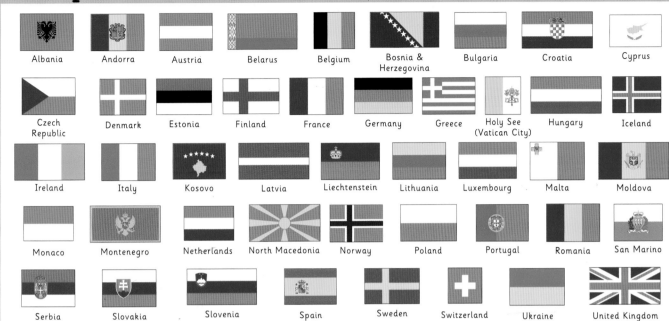

Albania	Andorra	Austria	Belarus	Belgium	Bosnia & Herzegovina	Bulgaria	Croatia	Cyprus
Czech Republic	Denmark	Estonia	Finland	France	Germany	Greece	Holy See (Vatican City)	Hungary	Iceland
Ireland	Italy	Kosovo	Latvia	Liechtenstein	Lithuania	Luxembourg	Malta	Moldova
Monaco	Montenegro	Netherlands	North Macedonia	Norway	Poland	Portugal	Romania	San Marino
Serbia	Slovakia	Slovenia	Spain	Sweden	Switzerland	Ukraine	United Kingdom

Asia

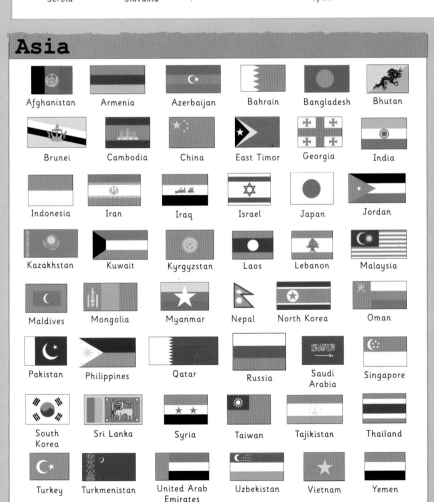

Afghanistan	Armenia	Azerbaijan	Bahrain	Bangladesh	Bhutan
Brunei	Cambodia	China	East Timor	Georgia	India
Indonesia	Iran	Iraq	Israel	Japan	Jordan
Kazakhstan	Kuwait	Kyrgyzstan	Laos	Lebanon	Malaysia
Maldives	Mongolia	Myanmar	Nepal	North Korea	Oman
Pakistan	Philippines	Qatar	Russia	Saudi Arabia	Singapore
South Korea	Sri Lanka	Syria	Taiwan	Tajikistan	Thailand
Turkey	Turkmenistan	United Arab Emirates	Uzbekistan	Vietnam	Yemen

The study of flags is called VEXILLOLOGY.

Oceania

Australia	Federated States of Micronesia	Fiji
Kiribati	Marshall Islands	Nauru
New Zealand	Palau	Papua New Guinea
Samoa	Solomon Islands	Tonga
Tuvalu	Vanuatu	

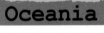

131

The natural

world

From lush forests and winding rivers, to hidden caves and massive mountains, our world is brimming with incredible **natural wonders**. Are you ready to hike through a rainforest, crawl through a spooky cave, and relax in a natural hot spring?

Oceans and seas

The oceans are the five largest **areas of seawater** on Earth. They are all connected to each other. Smaller areas of seawater are called seas.

Arctic Ocean

The Pacific is the world's largest and deepest ocean. It contains more than half of all the liquid water on Earth!

Pacific Ocean

I'm a marine biologist. It's my job to study life in our amazing oceans.

Underwater gardens

The oceans and seas are full of fascinating animals and plants. Plants provide homes for the animals and food for them to eat.

The Arctic is the smallest ocean. It surrounds the North Pole and most of it is covered in ice, especially during winter.

Arctic Ocean

Atlantic Ocean

Pacific Ocean

Indian Ocean

The Atlantic is the second largest ocean. It separates the Americas from Europe and Africa.

The Indian Ocean is the warmest ocean. It is the area of water between Africa and Australia.

The Southern Ocean is also known as the Antarctic Ocean. It's the only ocean that goes all the way round the globe.

Southern Ocean

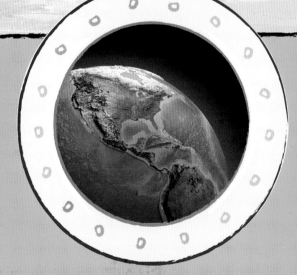

Ocean view
From space, the Earth looks blue because the oceans and seas cover much more of its surface than land does. That's why Earth is sometimes called "**the blue planet**".

135

Geysers and hot springs

Geysers and hot springs are places where hot water from beneath the earth finds a way **out of the ground**. Look out, they're hot!

Hot springs

Hot springs are places where water that is warmed by heat from under the earth escapes through cracks in the ground and **forms pools or rivers** of hot water.

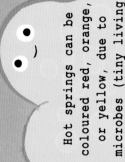

Hot springs can be coloured red, orange, or yellow, due to microbes (tiny living things) in the water.

Geyser

Hot spring →

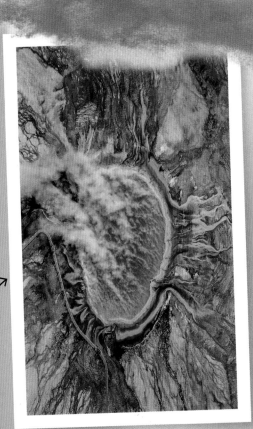

Geysers

Some hot springs have water that boils and then shoots up **like an erupting volcano**! But instead of lava, it's jets of water and steam that are being shot into the air. These places are called geysers.

136

Volcanic gases can cause some hot springs to smell like rotten eggs!

Look out, that's HOT!

Jigokudani Monkey Park in Japan is home to wild Japanese macaques. The monkeys love to relax together in the natural hot springs there.

This beautiful hot spring in Iceland, "The Blue Lagoon" is actually man-made. The water is kept at the perfect temperature for bathing.

Old Faithful, USA, is a world-famous geyser that erupts every one to two hours. People used to wash clothes in the hot water.

Forests

Grizzly bears

Around a third of the Earth's land is covered in forests. Trees provide a **home** for millions of animals, and even clean the air that we breathe.

Boreal forests are found in colder parts of the world. Boreal forests have short summers and long, cold winters.

Banff National Park contains part of Canada's boreal forest. Its lakes and glaciers are spectacular.

Great Smoky Mountains National Park, USA, is a temperate forest. Hundreds of different types of trees can be found there.

Temperate forests are found in more mild climates. They change a lot across all four seasons. The word temperate means "not extreme".

Raccoon

Toucan

Tropical rainforests

are warm and humid with lots of rainfall. They only have two seasons: a rainy season and a dry season.

Jaguars are one of the Amazon's top predators.

The Amazon Rainforest is the largest tropical forest in the world. Most of it is in Brazil, but parts are in Peru, Colombia, and other countries.

Rainforests have four layers, each with its own unique wildlife:

Emergent layer

Canopy

Understorey

Forest floor

Jaguar

More than half of the world's species of plants and animals are found in rainforests.

Deserts

Places that get very little **rainfall** are called deserts. Only plants and animals that don't need much water can live in deserts.

Our feathers keep us warm in the icy desert!

Not all deserts are hot. It almost never rains in Antarctica, making it one big desert!

The Sahara Desert in Africa is the biggest desert on Earth. It's about the size of the USA!

Desert animals have

Camel

Camels have one or two humps. Storing fat in their humps helps them to go without food or water for weeks!

Jerboa

Tiny jerboas have long and powerful legs, which are useful for digging, jumping, and running away from enemies.

Clever cacti

Cacti collect water when it rains and **store** it in their stems. This is what allows them to survive in deserts.

Lots of dinosaur fossils have been found in the Gobi Desert in Asia.

Strangely shaped rocks are formed in deserts after years of very strong winds.

SPECIAL FEATURES that help them survive.

Lizard

Many lizards burrow in the sand to escape from enemies and the heat. Their scaly feet stop them from sinking when they scurry across the sand.

Fennec fox

Many desert animals, including the fennec fox, sleep underground during the day and explore the desert at night when it is cooler.

Mountains

Plates

Mountains and volcanoes both look like spiky rocks reaching into the sky. But what's the **difference**?

Mountains

The Earth's crust (the ground you stand on) is made up of different **giant plates**. These slowly move and sometimes crash together. Over millions of years, this forces the ground upward, forming mountains.

Most mountains are part of ranges such as the Alps or the Himalayas. Mountain ranges can spread for thousands of miles.

Mount Kilimanjaro
Africa's highest peak can be found in Tanzania. Kilimanjaro is a dormant volcano, which means it hasn't erupted in a long time.

Mauna Kea
Located in Hawaii, USA, Mauna Kea is the tallest mountain in the world. However, most of it is underwater, so its peak isn't as high as other mountains.

and Volcanoes

Volcanoes

Volcanoes are openings in the Earth that fiery rock can **erupt** from. When volcanoes erupt, lava, ash, and dust is shot into the air.

Many volcanoes are located under the sea. Eruptions from these volcanoes can create new islands!

What is lava?

Lava is melted rock from deep within the Earth that has erupted from a volcano. It's extremely hot and destructive. When this rock is still inside the volcano, it's called magma.

Lava

Magma

Mount Vesuvius
This active volcano in Naples, Italy has erupted many times. In the year 79 it erupted and covered the city of Pompeii in ash.

Eyjafjallajökull
In 2010, this volcano in Iceland erupted and shot an enormous cloud of ash into the sky. This caused chaos for air travel.

Caves

Caves are holes that go deep **underground**.
People used to shelter in caves in prehistoric times,
and many animals live in them today.

Stalactite

How are caves created?

In most cases, caves form naturally over
millions of years. Rainwater seeps
into cracks in certain types of rock and
wears it away bit by bit. This happens
because rainwater is slightly acidic.

Stalagmite

Speleothems

Spiky rocks

Many caves have spiky mineral formations
called speleothems. The main ones are
stalagmites, which grow up from
the floor, and **stalactites**, which
hang from the cave ceiling.

Cave dwellers

Some animals have adapted to live in the **darkness** of caves. Blind albino cave crabs live in caves in the Canary Islands, and many bats like dark and quiet places.

Amazing caves

Hang Sơn Đoòng, Vietnam
This is the biggest cave in the world. It's so big there is a forest, river, and even clouds inside.

In a cave in Kantemó, Mexico, yellow-red rat snakes who usually live on the forest floor hang from the ceiling and try to catch bats!

Albino cave crab

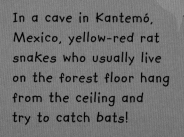

People who explore caves are called "spelunkers".

Fingal's Cave, Scotland
Formed more than 50 million years ago by lava, this cave is famous for its shape and the way things sound inside it.

Orda Cave, Russia
This is one of the longest underwater caves in the world. Its crystal clear waters make it a dream for scuba divers.

Dobšinská Ice Cave, Slovakia
The ice in this famous cave is incredibly thick. Visitors can take a tour of the cave and see it for themselves.

Lakes

Lakes are large pools of water **surrounded by land**. They can be absolutely huge and full of life, or mostly lifeless.

How are lakes made?

Lakes are formed when **basins** (pits) fill with water. The water comes from rain or melted ice from glaciers.

Swan ↰

Animals need fresh water to survive, so lots of animals live in or near lakes.

Otter →

Heron ↰

The world's biggest lake

In-between Europe and Asia is the biggest lake in the world, the **Caspian Sea**. It's so big that people used to think it was an ocean! It became separated from the Mediterranean Sea more than 5 million years ago when the Earth's crust moved.

Caspian sea ↗

Life on Mars

In 2018, scientists found evidence of an **underground lake** on Mars. The discovery might help us understand what happened to the water that once covered the planet. It may even mean life can exist there!

Dragonfly ↘

Freshwater trout

Toad ↘

Newt ↘

Lake Hillier

Duck ↘

Salt lakes

Lakes that contain lots of salt are very unusual. Sometimes, tiny creatures called **bacteria** grow in very salty lakes. These creatures can turn lakes, such as Lake Hillier in Australia, pink!

The Dead Sea
Don't let the name confuse you! The Dead Sea is a giant lake with water so salty that almost nothing can live in it. The salt makes it very easy to float on the water.

Lake Baikal
This lake in Russia is around four times as deep as New York's Empire State Building is tall – making it the deepest lake on Earth. It's also the world's biggest source of fresh water.

Lake Vostok
You wouldn't want to go for a swim in this lake! It's located underneath the Antarctic ice sheet, where the ice is up to 4 km (2.5 miles) thick!

Rivers

When fresh water flows from a mountain or hill, a trickling stream is formed. Lots of streams join up to make a river, which **twists and turns** all the way to the sea.

There are more than **3,000** species

Wildlife

Rivers are filled with wildlife, **especially fish**. Animals such as birds and bears are drawn to the fish-filled waters for food. Humans also like to go fishing in rivers.

The Amazon contains animals such as dolphins and piranhas!

Piranha

Pink river dolphin

The mighty Amazon

The Amazon River cuts through the Amazon **Rainforest** in South America. It carries more water than any other river on Earth. Its mouth is nearly as wide as the distance between London and Paris!

of fish in the Amazon River!

The longest river in the world is the River Nile. It flows through 11 countries in Africa.

Life of a river

Rainwater and melted snow flow into streams.

Stream

River

Small streams join together and form a river.

Dam

Some rivers have dams that slow the flow of water.

River mouth

The river slows down when it joins the sea.

Waterfalls

When a river reaches a steep drop, it falls over the edge to a pool below, creating a beautiful sheet of **rushing water**, called a waterfall.

Which type?

There are many different types of waterfall. Some plunge **straight down** to the pool below, whilst others fall down a **series of steps** made out of rocks.

Yosemite Falls
USA: 739m (2,425ft)

Sutherland Falls
New Zealand: 580m (1,904ft)

Sutherland Falls drops down three big steps before reaching the pool below.

A trick of the light makes it look like Yosemite Falls is burning at certain times!

Angel Falls
Venezuela: 979m (3,212ft)

Angel Falls is the world's tallest waterfall. It's more than twice the height of New York's Empire State Building!

How are they made?

Waterfalls are created by the process of **erosion**. Over time, the river wears away the rock beneath it. This creates a sharp ledge that the water falls over.

In winter, some waterfalls freeze and form huge icicles.

Some daring people go over waterfalls for fun. In 1901, Annie Taylor became the first person to survive the drop over Niagara Falls in a barrel!

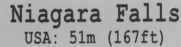

Niagara Falls
USA: 51m (167ft)

Plains

Imagine being able to see for miles and miles in all directions. That's what the view is like on plains: wide, open flatlands that stretch as **far as the eye can see**.

Wildebeest

Care to ex-plain?

Plains are **very flat** areas of land. There are several types including grasslands, forests, savannas, and even underwater plains. Most plains have extreme weather such as strong winds, hot summers, and dry, cold winters.

The Serengeti

The Serengeti plains in TANZANIA and KENYA are some of the most spectacular in the world.

On the move

The Serengeti is a grassland that experiences very dry summers. Every year, millions of wildebeest, zebras, and gazelles **travel across** the vast plains in search of fresh grass, water, and a safe place to have babies.

Plains can be formed by erosion, volcanic eruptions, and floods.

The Serengeti is known to locals as "the land that goes on forever".

There are plains all over, and out of, the world!

The Great Plains
These wide grasslands in North America are mostly used for farming. Watch out for "Tornado Alley" and its frequent and dangerous tornadoes.

Arctic plains
Plains in the Arctic are called "tundra". These largely treeless areas have long, cold winters that are spent in almost total darkness.

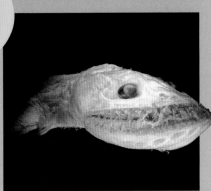

Under the sea
Believe it or not, there are underwater plains in the deepest oceans. The plains are filled with strange fish and other marine animals.

Out of this world
Planets such as Mercury and Mars have plains, too. Several spacecraft and rovers have landed on Mars and explored the surface.

Perfect plants

The world is filled with billions of **plants**. From tiny flowers to towering trees, plants come in all shapes, sizes, and colours.

Fantastic flowers

Flowers are beautiful, but they also help the plant make new seeds. Flowers also provide **food and shelter** for animals.

Leaves

Plants need light, water, nutrients, and air to grow properly.

Bees are attracted to bright flowers. They collect nectar from plants and turn it into honey.

Sunflower

FLOWERS

Orchid   Daffodils   Tulips

HERBS AND SPICES

Chives   Chillis   Mint

Plants make the OXYGEN that we breathe.

I tap into tree trunks to find tasty insects to eat. I also make holes that are perfect for nesting in!

Woodpecker

Trunk

Terrific trees

Trees have a thick **trunk** connected to the roots underground. The trunk gets taller and thicker to hold the tree up as it grows bigger.

FRUITS AND VEGETABLES

Tomatoes   Potatoes   Strawberries   Cucumbers

TREES

Evergreen trees, like pine trees, keep their leaves all year round!

Deciduous trees such as oak trees lose their leaves in the autumn.

Fruit trees, such as apple trees, grow fruit that we can eat.

Many trees, such as the cherry blossom, produces flowers.

There are more than **300,000** types of plants.

I'm a mammal!

Wildlife

Our world is filled with **amazing animals**! From enormous elephants to slithering snakes, each animal is special in its own way.

Mammals

All mammals have **warm blood**, similar skeletons, and almost all have hair. Humans are mammals, too!

Elephant

Bat

I'm an underwater mammal!

Dolphin

Birds

Although not all birds can fly, they all have **feathers**, a beak, and they all hatch from eggs.

Parrot

I can't fly, but I'm a fast runner!

Emu

Duck

Fish

Fish live underwater. They breathe using gills and swim with fins. Most fish have scales and **cold blood**.

Shark

Seahorse

Angelfish

The animal groups

There are many **different types** of animals so scientists sort them into **six big groups**. This helps us understand the differences and similarities between animals.

Did you know that most of the world's animals have no bones? We are called invertebrates.

Reptiles

Reptiles are covered in **scales** and shed their skin. Most reptiles have cold blood and they almost all hatch from eggs.

Snake

Alligator

Lizard

Amphibians

Most amphibians spend some of their lives in the **water**, and some on **land**. They hatch from eggs in water, have cold blood, and slippery skin.

Caecilian

Salamander

Arthropods

The **biggest** animal group is the arthropods, which is made up of insects, arachnids, and crustaceans. They all have **lots of legs**!

Ladybird

Butterfly

Lobster

157

Exploring

the world

The big wide world is just waiting to be explored!
From tall towers to breathtakingly beautiful buildings,
there are countless amazing attractions to experience.
All you have to do is turn the page to set off on a
big adventure!

Huacachina

In the Peruvian desert, where water is precious, this amazing town is built around an **oasis**. People travel to Huacachina in search of adventure.

A town in the desert

The town of Huacachina (pronounced "whaka-cheena") is a few hours away from Peru's capital, Lima. It's surrounded on all sides by **massive sand dunes.**

Only around 100 people live in Huacachina, but thousands of tourists travel there each year.

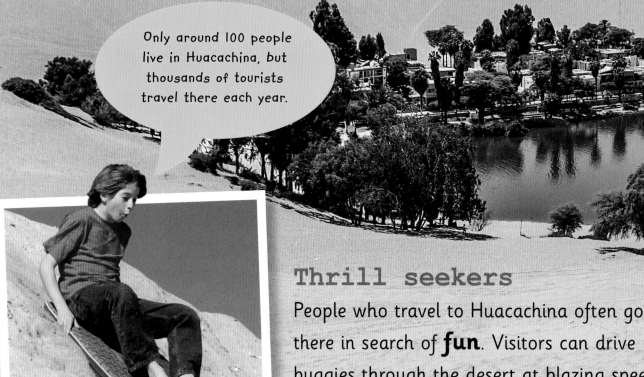

Thrill seekers

People who travel to Huacachina often go there in search of **fun**. Visitors can drive buggies through the desert at blazing speed, or go sandboarding across the sand dunes!

Nazca Lines

Found a short distance from Huacachina, the mysterious Nazca Lines are huge shapes and **animal drawings** that were scratched into the land by the Ancient Nazca people thousands of years ago.

Huacachina means "WEEPING WOMAN". Legend has it that the lake is filled with the tears of a princess.

Tulip fields

Tulips are the national flower of the Netherlands. Beautiful **fields** filled with rows of the colourful flowers can be found across the country.

Black tulips were a myth for hundreds of years, but in 1986 the first was grown.

The best time to see the tulip fields is between March and May, when the flowers are in full bloom.

Tulip mad!

Tulips were introduced to the Netherlands in the 1500s from Turkey. They were so popular that this time became known as "Tulipomania". People bought tulip bulbs with gold and others stole them from gardens!

The word tulip comes from the Turkish word "tulipan", which means "turban".

With over 7 million flowers and 800 types of tulip on display, the yearly **Keukenhof flower festival** in Lisse, is one of the biggest flower exhibits in the world.

The Dutch have a **national tulip day** every year. Flower parades take place and the main square in Amsterdam is filled with tulips for people to pick for free from a special garden.

Neuschwanstein castle

On top of a hill in the mountains of Bavaria, Germany, sits this stunningly **beautiful castle**.

The castle at Walt Disney's Magic Kingdom theme park is based on Neuschwanstein.

The castle has a huge inner garden and more than 100 rooms, many of which are filled with intricate paintings, carvings, and furniture.

A fairytale castle

Most castles are built to protect against attackers, but Neuschwanstein was just built to **look amazing**. That's why it looks like it belongs in a fairy tale.

Images of swans appear around the castle because swans appeared in Ludwig's favourite legends.

Neuschwanstein is pronounced "NOY-shvan-stine".

Ludwig II

The castle was built in 1886. The ruler of Bavaria at the time was Ludwig II. He had expensive taste and a love of myths, stories, and **legends**. Ludwig wanted to live in a castle that was like the ones from his stories – so he had one built!

It took 18 years to build Ludwig's dream castle, but he only got to live there for 172 days!

The Eden Project

Step into the incredible **world of trees and plants** at the Eden Project in Cornwall, UK. Its gardens and greenhouse domes are home to nearly two million plants.

The Mediterranean seaside biome is very hot in summer but rainy and cool in winter.

What's a biome?
Places throughout the world that share similar climates, plants, and wildlife are known as biomes.

Rainforests are a hot and rainy biome.

The Eden Project houses the LARGEST

Walk through the rainforest

In the **tropical** heat of the rainforest greenhouse, you can see banana and cacao trees, fragrant orchids, and even a gushing waterfall.

Australian grass tree

The giant flower, Titan arum, smells like rotting meat! When it opens its petals, it attracts insects from far and wide.

Titan arum

Experience the Mediterranean

Smell fresh herbs and plants in the **warm** Mediterranean greenhouse. You'll also find Western Australian grass trees, gnarly cork sculptures, and a golden mosaic path.

The gardens

Outside of the greenhouse domes are thousands of flowers growing in the fresh air, as well as **allotments** growing food from around the world.

This huge sculpture was created by Robert Bradford to remind visitors of the importance of bees in nature.

INDOOR RAINFOREST in the world.

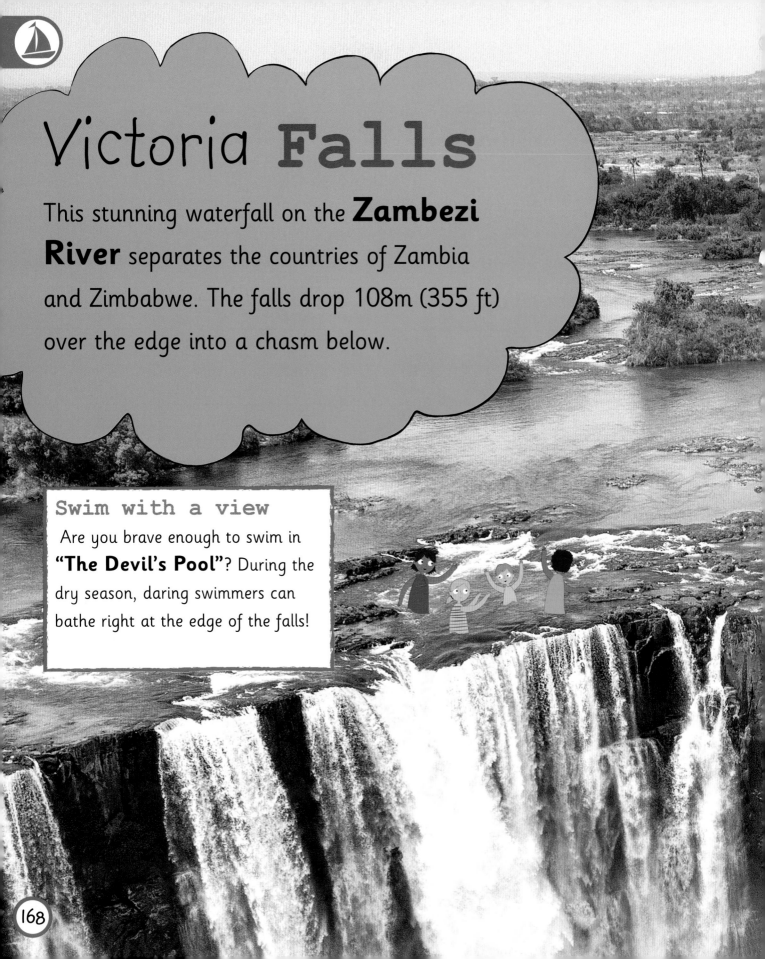

Victoria Falls

This stunning waterfall on the **Zambezi River** separates the countries of Zambia and Zimbabwe. The falls drop 108m (355 ft) over the edge into a chasm below.

Swim with a view

Are you brave enough to swim in **"The Devil's Pool"**? During the dry season, daring swimmers can bathe right at the edge of the falls!

The Zambezi River flows through six countries. Victoria Falls is just one of the waterfalls along the river's route.

Victoria falls is also called "Mosi-oa-Tunya", which means "THE SMOKE THAT THUNDERS"

Most of Africa was a mystery to the rest of the world when the **explorer** David Livingstone first visited the continent. He was the first European to see the falls, and named them after Queen Victoria of the UK.

Uluru

This giant **sacred rock**, found deep in the Australian desert (bush), is named Uluru. It is owned by the Anangu people, and is home to tens of thousands of years of living history.

In Anangu stories, the curves and marks in the rock are said to have been made by an ANGRY SNAKE.

Bush food

Even in the emptiness of the bush, there is food if you know where to look. Anangu people know how to **hunt** and **gather** fruit, meat, and grubs.

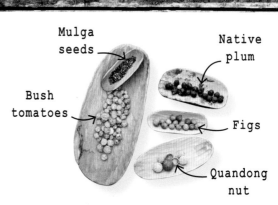

Mulga seeds

Native plum

Bush tomatoes

Figs

Quandong nut

The sacred rock

Inside Uluru is a series of caves, filled with **ancient rock art**. These artworks pass down Anangu knowledge, stories, and responsibilities through generations.

Some rock art was drawn on top of other pictures because the cave walls were used like a teacher's whiteboard to tell Anangu stories.

The giant rock extends a long way under ground.

Wildlife

The Australian bush is filled with animals and plants that are **specially adapted** to living in the hot, dry desert.

Thorny devil

Hare wallaby

171

The Taj Mahal

One of the most beautiful buildings in the world can be found in northern India. It took more than 20 years of work and nearly 20,000 workers to build this spectacular **mausoleum.**

The large central dome is surrounded by four smaller ones.

The palace was built for Mughal emperor Shah Jahan in memory of his beloved wife Mumtaz Mahal.

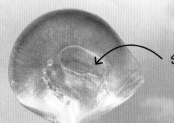

Some walls are decorated with mother of pearl – a shiny substance found in oysters.

The perfect palace

The Taj Mahal is famous for its **symmetry** – it looks the same from every side! It's decorated with white marble and dozens of precious stones.

Taj Mahal means "Crown of Palaces."

The palace reflects light and appears to change colour depending on the time of day or season you visit.

Smile for the camera

The palace is visited by almost a **million tourists every year**. Thousands of them recreate the same photograph with the magnificent palace behind them – **say cheese!**

What an amazing building!

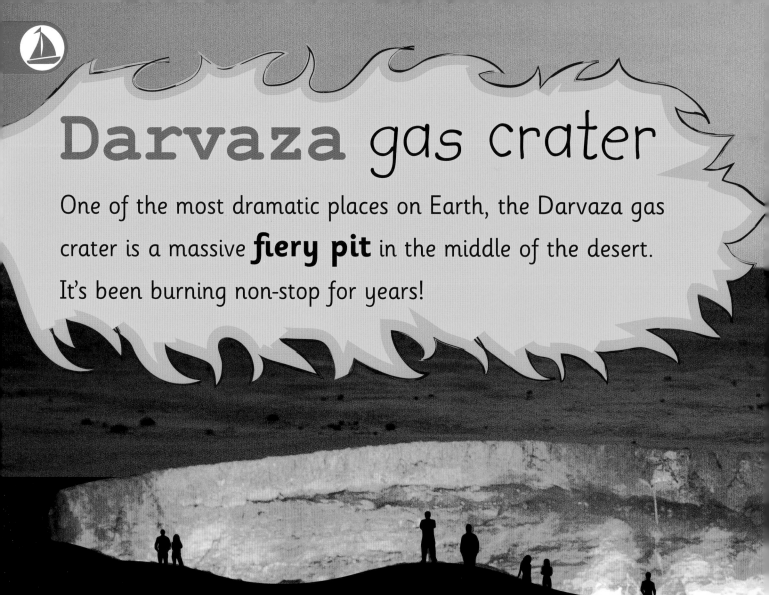

Darvaza gas crater

One of the most dramatic places on Earth, the Darvaza gas crater is a massive **fiery pit** in the middle of the desert. It's been burning non-stop for years!

Although the crater is isolated in the desert, people have come from far and wide to see it. There's nothing else there, not even a safety rail!

How did it get there?

In 1971, a group of scientists were drilling in the **Karakum Desert** in Turkmenistan. The ground collapsed, revealing a huge underground cave filled with methane gas. They set the crater on fire to get rid of the gas, thinking it would soon burn out. They were wrong! It's been burning ever since!

The crater is 69 m (226 ft) wide, and 30 metres (98 ft) deep.

This giant crater is also known as "The Door to Hell".

Daredevil

The temperature inside is more than ten times hotter than boiling water! In 2014, the explorer George Kourounis became the first person to **climb down into the pit** and walk across it.

George Kourounis's journey into the pit was very dangerous. He had to wear very special equipment to protect himself from the heat.

The lost city of Petra

More than 2,000 years ago, the ancient city of Petra was carved straight into a cliff. This hidden city was abandoned, forgotten, then found again **hundreds of years** later.

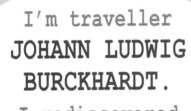

I'm traveller **JOHANN LUDWIG BURCKHARDT**. I rediscovered Petra in 1812.

Petra is also known as the "Rose City" because the sandstone cliff it is carved into looks pink.

Petra was once a **WEALTHY CITY** where spices were traded.

The city was set up by the **Nabataean people**. Although they were nomads who travelled around the desert, Petra became their capital.

Petra is located in **Jordan**. At the time of the Nabataeans, merchants crossed the Arabian Desert on **camels** to reach it.

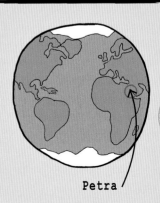

Petra

Petra is hidden at the end of the Siq, a long, narrow path through the cliffs.

Socotra

What is it like on the "the most **alien** place on Earth"? You'd have to visit this island off the coast of Yemen to find out.

Desert rose

Socotra is sometimes called "The Island of Bliss".

Socotra

Unusual island

Many of the plants and many of the animals found on the island can't be found **anywhere else** on Earth – and don't look like anything else on Earth either!

The reason plants and animals on Socotra are so unique is because the island has been separated from mainland Africa for more than 6 million years.

Africa

Egyptian vulture

178

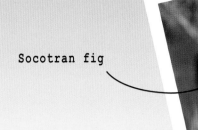
Socotran fig

Bottle tree

About 60,000 people live on Socotra, but there are almost no roads.

Monarch chameleon

Dragon blood tree

This tree's shape isn't the only unusual thing about it – the bark **bleeds** a blood-red sap, which can be used as a dye, or as a medicine to treat cuts, bites, and burns.

Dragon blood tree

Although it looks like an inside-out umbrella, the tree's shape helps it collect water, not repel it.

Hitachi Seaside Park

This magical place in Hitachinaka, Japan, is always colourful. Hitachi Seaside Park is in **bloom all year long**, so visitors can stroll through a rainbow of plants and flowers.

Summer

Over the summer months, four and a half million Nemophila, or "baby blue eyes" bloom in the park.

Autumn

On Miharashi Hill, Kochia herbs turn from lush green in the summer to a fiery red colour in the autumn.

Blooming rainbow

From a sea of blue Nemophila in spring, to a carpet of red Kochia in autumn, different flowers bloom as the **seasons** change.

Winter

Late winter and early spring see the arrival of masses of golden yellow daffodils.

Spring

In spring, the park's woodlands are filled with rows of brightly coloured tulips.

Giant's Causeway

These stepping-stone like **columns of rock** off the northern coast of Ireland are so unusual, they're famous all over the world. But how did they get there?

Spectacular stones

Around 60 million years ago, liquid rock erupted from the Earth's crust. Eventually, the liquid rock cooled, turned solid, and **cracked**, splitting into thousands of columns, most of them with six sides.

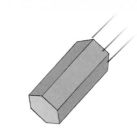

The columns are made of a rock called basalt. There are around 40,000 of them!

A giant story

According to an Irish legend, a giant called Finn MacCool built the causeway as a **bridge** across the sea to Scotland so that he could fight one of his enemies.

The causeway is home to lots of birds and rare plants.

One throne-shaped section of rock is called the Wishing Chair. In the past only women could sit there.

Mount Everest

At 8,848m (29,029 ft), Mount Everest in Asia is the **highest point on Earth**. The views from the top are amazing, but reaching the peak is a real achievement!

It takes around 2 MONTHS to climb Mount Everest.

Climbers stop off at a base camp part of the way up the mountain, to prepare for the most difficult part of the trek.

Oxygen tank

Warm clothing

The climb

Everest is bitterly cold, dangerously steep, and so high there's barely any **oxygen**. Over the years, many people have climbed it, but most don't reach the top. It's almost impossible without oxygen tanks.

← The peak

Memorable mountaineers

In 1953, Sir Edmund Hillary and Tenzing Norgay became the **first people** to reach the top of Mount Everest.

Sherpas

The Sherpas are a group of people that live at the base of Everest. They act as **guides** and help visiting climbers go up the mountain.

The Great Wall of China

While China has many modern cities, one of its most famous sights is a huge wall built more than **2,000 years ago**.

The Great Wall is the largest man-made structure on Earth!

Building the wall

The Great Wall wasn't built all at once. Several shorter walls were **connected together** and added to over many years. It is thought to have once been around 8,850km (5,500 miles) long. Today, much of the wall has crumbled into ruin, but it's still huge!

The wall is made from stone, earth, and sticks. Its average height is taller than a giraffe.

Ancient China

Long ago, China used to be split into several warring states. Qin Shi Huang, the ruler of one of these states, conquered his enemies. He united China as one country and became its **first Emperor**.

The Great Wall is now one of China's most popular tourist destinations. More than 10 million people visit it each year.

Soldiers guarded sections of the wall from watchtowers.

Qin Shi Huang

Qin Shi Huang had the walls joined up to protect China from foreign **invaders**. Hundreds of thousands of workers spent years building it and making repairs.

Many people claim the Great Wall is visible from space, but this isn't true.

Pompeii

It may be impossible to go back in time, but this ancient city in Italy has been **frozen in time**. A visit here is like taking a trip to the past.

People who study ancient objects and sites are called archaeologists. Archaeologists dug through nearly 5m (16ft) of ash to uncover Pompeii.

What happened?

The city of Pompeii is located near the volcano **Mount Vesuvius**. In the year 79, Vesuvius erupted, wiping out the town and burying it under a heap of ash for almost 2,000 years.

Coins

Mount Vesuvius

Mount Vesuvius is an active volcano. It could erupt again!

When Vesuvius erupted, it took just two hours for the town to be totally buried in ash, rock, and lava.

The ash preserved Pompeii. Today you can visit and explore the ruins.

Preserved villa

Ancient food shop

Attractions:

- ✓ Wander down a Roman street
- ✓ Visit some Roman baths
- ✓ Find a mosaic fountain
- ✓ Stand in a preserved villa
- ✓ Look for a temple
- ✓ Admire the amphitheatre

The Great Barrier Reef

This giant coral reef off the coast of Australia is one of the most incredible places in the natural world. It is bursting with colourful plants and creatures, but it is **under threat**.

What is a coral reef?
Made from skeletal remains and minerals, a coral reef is **home** to lots of plants and animals that live underwater.

Disappearing reef

Due to climate change, oceans are becoming warmer. This can cause **coral bleaching**, which destroys coral. A huge amount of the Great Barrier Reef has been bleached, and as a result, the habitat that millions of creatures rely on is disappearing.

The Great Barrier Reef is made up of more than 2,900 reefs and 900 islands. It's so big it can be seen from space.

Conservation

Scientists are growing coral to try to save the reef. By reducing our **carbon footprint** (the amount of carbon dioxide gas released into the air), we can help, too.

Conservationists work to come up with ways to save coral.

191

Christmas Island

Every year, something incredible happens on this little island in the Indian Ocean. Millions of **red crabs** come out of the forest and head to the beach together.

Festive name

On Christmas Day in 1643, William Mynors, a captain in the East India Company, sailed past the island and gave it its unique name.

ROAD CLOSED

Local rangers set up special paths, bridges, and tunnels, and close some roads to protect the crabs from cars during their journey.

Around 40 to 50 million red crabs gather on the beach at once.

The reason these crabs make their way to the ocean is to make **baby crabs**. The males arrive first and meet the females on the beach.

1

When the tide is just right, the female crabs lay their eggs and release them into the ocean.

2

The tiny *baby crabs* spend a month in the ocean *before* returning to land.

3

The crabs then travel to the centre of the island and shelter in the forest until they are grown.

The Burj Khalifa is 828 m (2,716 ft) tall.

The tower is so huge it can be seen from 100 km (60 miles) away.

1st

The tower holds several world records, including tallest building in the world.

Burj Khalifa

Some of the most **spectacular buildings** in the world can be found in Dubai, United Arab Emirates. But none are more impressive than the Burj Khalifa.

Record breaker

The Burj Khalifa is a record breaker in more ways than one. It weighs more than 100,000 elephants, has the **most floors** of any building **in the world**, and has the highest restaurant and swimming pool.

There are more than 1,000 apartments, offices, and hotel rooms inside the tower.

The Burj Khalifa is among the MOST PHOTOGRAPHED buildings in the world.

Discover Dubai

The city of Dubai is full of **incredible buildings** and structures.

These giant artificial islands were made in the shape of a tree. They are called the **Palm Islands.**

With more than 1,200 shops, **Dubai Mall** is the world's biggest shopping centre.

The mountains are located in a place in China called Zhangye Danxia Geopark. Danxia means "rosy clouds".

Kaleidoscope of colour

The colours come from **minerals** in the rock. When it rains, the water mixes with the different types of rock and changes their colour. It's similar to the process of metal turning red and rusty in the rain.

Rainbow Mountains

Have you ever dreamed of walking on a **rainbow**? The closest thing to that might be visiting China's naturally rainbow-coloured mountains and going for a hike!

The mountains are 80 MILLION YEARS OLD!

The crumbled look of the mountains comes from movement in Earth's crust.

Mystery mountains

The Rainbow Mountains are very **remote** and hardly anyone had heard of them before the year 2000. After photos of the mountains became famous, travellers from all over the globe began to visit.

The best time of year to see the Northern Lights is the winter, when the skies are darkest.

Auroras

If you look up at the sky at the right time in certain parts of the world, you might see colourful dancing lights above you. This amazing effect is called an **aurora.**

What causes auroras?

Auroras happen when particles from the Sun called **solar winds** slam into the Earth's magnetic field. These particles hit tiny things in the air called atoms and make them light up.

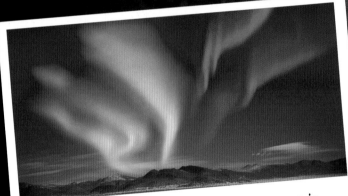

The most common colour for an aurora is green, but they also appear as red, pink, yellow, and blue.

Duelling dragons

A **Chinese legend** says auroras were caused by good and evil dragons duelling in the sky.

Fire foxes

According to a **Finnish myth**, auroras were caused by the tails of foxes made of fire that streak through the sky.

Room with a view

Canada, Alaska, and Northern Europe are all great places to see auroras. Northern Lights Village in Finland is one of the best places to view the dazzling light display. You can stay in cabins with glass ceilings and watch the amazing spectacle from bed!

Displays near the North Pole are known as Aurora Borealis, or northern lights.

By the South Pole, they are called Aurora Australis.

Telescopes have shown that Jupiter, Saturn, Uranus, and Neptune also have aurora displays.

Cave of the Crystals

Underground and out of sight in Mexico, something amazing has slowly been growing: a cave full of seriously impressive **giant crystals.**

A crystal palace

These crystals are found in a cave in Naica Mine in Mexico known as "Cueva de los Cristales". The cave is located **deep underground** and is extremely hot and humid.

The cave was flooded when it was discovered in 2000. When scientists drained the water, the crystals stopped growing.

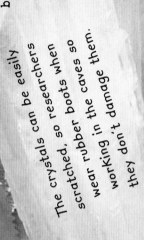

Rubber boots

The crystals can be easily scratched, so researchers wear rubber boots when working in the caves so they don't damage them.

These giant crystals are the largest in the world. They can weigh as much as eight elephants!

Breathing equipment

The largest crystals are 12m (39ft) long, which is longer than a London bus!

Researchers wear special suits and masks to protect them from the heat.

Protective suit

Giant gypsum

The crystals are made from a mineral called **gypsum**. Thousands of years of intense heat and humidity from below the Earth made them grow huge!

Another cave in Naica Mine called **"THE CAVE OF SWORDS"** is filled with small, spiky crystals!

Statue of Liberty

Standing tall and proud off the coast of New York City, USA, the Statue of Liberty represents hope and **freedom** across the world.

Signs and symbols

"Lady Liberty" was created to celebrate the American Revolution and the end of slavery in the USA. The statue faces towards the sea to welcome new arrivals to the USA, and is pictured stepping over **broken chains** to symbolise escaping the horrors of slavery.

Liberty's journey

The Statue of Liberty stands 93m (305 ft) tall from base to torch, and took over ten years to build in France. When she was done, she was shipped across the ocean in 214 wooden crates, reassembled, and finished in 1886.

My torch represents lighting the path towards freedom.

The statue was reddish-brown when it was first built. It turned green over time because of rain and oxygen.

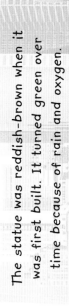

Broken chains

Ferry

Staten Island Ferry

Visitors can take a ferry to Liberty Island and see the statue up close.

Who made her?

The Statue of Liberty was a gift from the French people to the USA. It was designed by Frédéric-Auguste Bartholdi and built by Gustave Eiffel, who would go on to create the famous **Eiffel Tower** in Paris, France.

Frédéric-August Bartholdi

Gustave Eiffel

The Grand Canyon

Known for its incredible size, dramatic rock faces, and striking colours, the Grand Canyon, USA is one of the world's most **awe-inspiring landscapes**.

How did it get there?

Over millions of years the **Colorado River** cut into the Earth, gradually wearing away the rock little by little and creating a vast gorge.

Millions of people visit the **GRAND CANYON** every year.

The canyon has plenty of hiking trails, but they can be dangerous. Every year hundreds of hikers have to be rescued.

One of the best ways to take in the views is from the air. Helicopters take visitors on tours for the ultimate spectacle.

Very grand

The Grand Canyon is **enormous**! It's 446km (277 miles) long, 16km (10 miles) wide, and parts of it are so deep, the world's tallest building, the Burj Khalifa, would fit inside it with room to spare!

The Skywalk is a clear platform that allows visitors to look directly down into the canyon. It's not for the faint of heart!

There are lots of ways to take in the amazing sights!

The most daring adventurers can take an exhilarating trip down the river in a white-water raft!

Amundsen-Scott Station

Equipment, food, and other supplies have to be brought by boat or plane.

The South Pole is an icy **wilderness** with nothing around for miles and miles... except for this research station! What do you think it would be like to visit?

What happens here?

Nobody lives in Antarctica all the time, but **scientists** stay at the station and others to research and perform experiments on everything from the Earth and climate to wildlife, glaciers, and space.

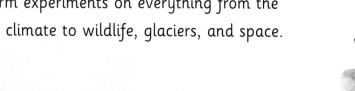

Robert Scott

206

Life at the station

Visitors to the base are usually there for a few months at a time. So in addition to the labs and living quarters, there's a dining hall, gym, games room, TV lounge, library, bar, hospital, post office, greenhouse, and shop. There's even a sauna!

Laboratory

Engineering

Living quarters

Roald Amundsen

The station is named after the explorers who led trips to the South Pole, Robert Scott from the UK and Roald Amundsen from Norway.

Antarctica is covered in ice, but there are still famous landmarks:

Most people who travel to Antarctica come through Drake Passage. It's one of the most stormy seas in the world.

Mount Erebus is Antarctica's most active volcano. It's a place where ice and fire meet.

The Ross Ice Shelf is named after the British Captain James Clark Ross. It's a block of ice about the size of France!

207

Easter Island

This isolated island in the middle of the Pacific Ocean is famous for something **hard to miss**: huge stone statues!

The biggest moai is a whopping 9m (30ft) tall!

Magnificent moai

887 statues, called **moai**, have stood on Easter Island for more than 500 years. The average height is 4m (13ft), which is nearly as tall as a giraffe!

Some of the statues are mostly buried underground.

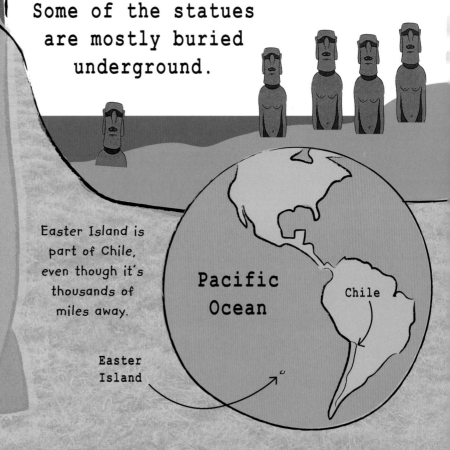

Easter Island is part of Chile, even though it's thousands of miles away.

Pacific Ocean

Chile

Easter Island

Ancient Polynesians sailed the Pacific looking for new islands.

Who carved them?

The moai were built by a group of people from Polynesia. Ancient Polynesians were amazing sailors who travelled thousands of miles on wooden canoes to explore the Pacific Ocean.

Most experts believe the moai were built to honour Polynesian ancestors.

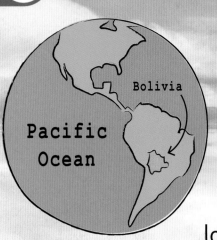

Pacific
Ocean

Bolivia

The Uyuni Salt Flats

Can you picture a place where the floor looks like a **mirror**? Because the Uyuni salt flats (Salar de Uyuni) in Bolivia is exactly that.

What are they?

The salt flats are an area that holds the world's largest inland collection of salt. When it rains, water floods the area, creating a **perfect reflection of the sky** on the ground.

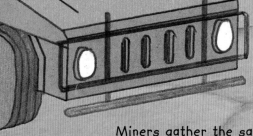

Miners gather the salt to be used for cooking and other uses.

It's hard to see where the ground stops and the sky begins!

THE SALT FLATS ARE THE FLATTEST PLACE ON EARTH!

Visitors to the salt flats can stay in special hotels where the furniture is made from blocks of salt!

Life on the flats

Most plants can't survive in salty ground, so there isn't much life on the flats. However, little rodents called **viscachas** survive on shrubs and cacti, and flocks of **flamingos** nest on the flats and wait for their eggs to hatch.

Viscacha

St. Basil's
Cathedral

In the centre of Russia's capital city, Moscow, stands one of the most recognizable, and **colourful**, buildings in the world. Just take a look at it!

Building St. Basil's

St. Basil's Cathedral was built on the orders of Ivan IV, the Tsar of Russia, or **Ivan the Terrible** as he is also known. When it was built between 1555 and 1561, it was the tallest building in Moscow.

Each dome has a unique pattern and colour.

Each chapel is topped with an onion-shaped dome.

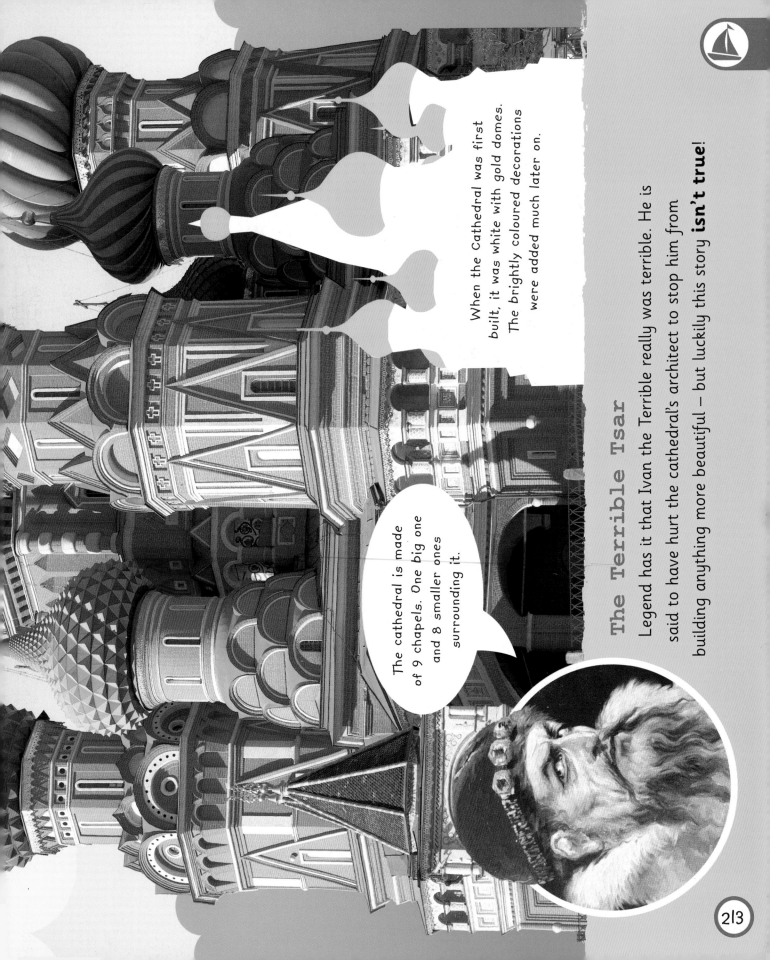

The cathedral is made of 9 chapels. One big one and 8 smaller ones surrounding it.

When the Cathedral was first built, it was white with gold domes. The brightly coloured decorations were added much later on.

The Terrible Tsar

Legend has it that Ivan the Terrible really was terrible. He is said to have hurt the cathedral's architect to stop him from building anything more beautiful – but luckily this story **isn't true**!

Eiffel Tower

Built in Paris, France, in 1889, the Eiffel Tower is one of the most famous buildings in the world. It's visited by **7 million** people a year!

Paris from above

The tower is 324m (1063 ft) tall, but the highest you can go up is 276m (906 ft). The viewing platform offers amazing views of the city, but it's a long way up – there are a staggering **1,710 steps** to climb!

The tower was built to celebrate the 100 year anniversary of the French Revolution.

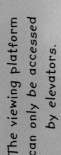

The viewing platform can only be accessed by elevators.

At night, the Eiffel tower becomes an incredible light show lit up with 20,000 bulbs!

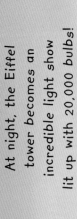

Building the tower

The enormous iron tower was designed by, and named after, Gustave Eiffel. With more than 18,000 parts, it took 300 workers around two years to build!

The second floor has a restaurant and shop with a spectacular view of Paris.

The first floor has a glass floor where visitors can look at the people below.

Gustave Eiffel

Not everyone liked the tower when it was built. Some protesters thought it LOOKED UGLY.

BOOO!

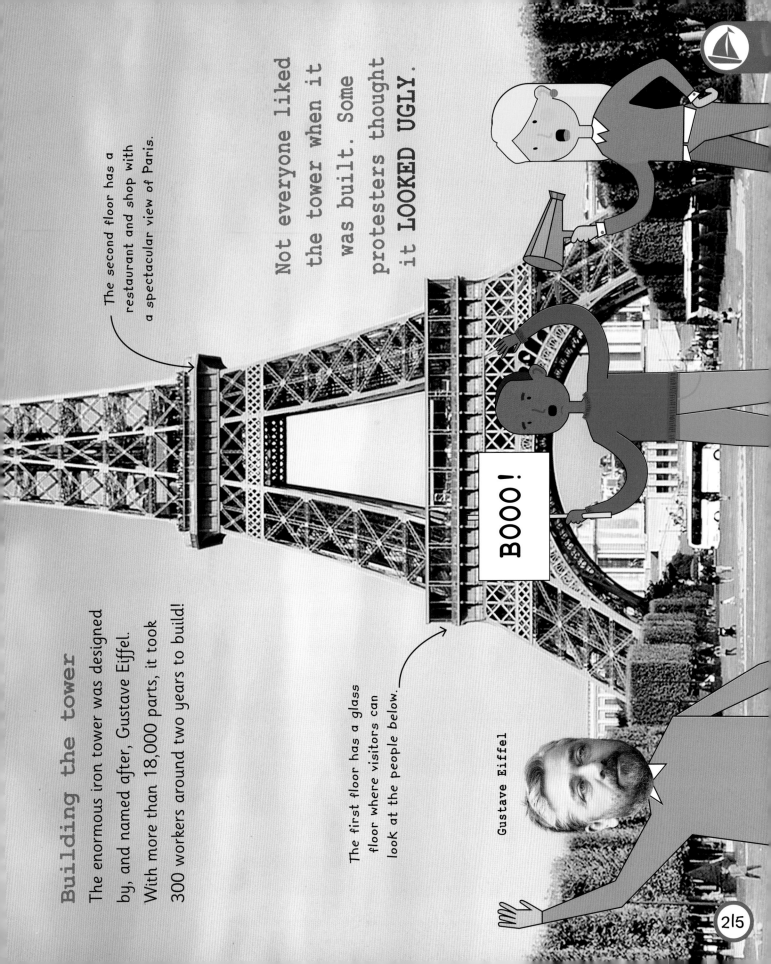

Sea of **Stars**

The Maldives is a nation in the Indian Ocean known for crystal clear water and beautiful beaches, but sometimes something mysterious occurs there that makes the **waves glow in the dark!**

Maldives

Indian
Ocean

The Maldives is made up of more than 1,000 islands. The glowing waves can happen around different islands, but is most common on Vaadhoo Island.

A similar version of this amazing spectacle can be seen on the island of Puerto Rico.

Pretty plankton

Despite its name, this sight isn't a reflection of the stars — it's created by tiny creatures called **plankton**. Some types of plankton can create their own light, which makes a beautiful glowing effect called **bioluminescence**.

A rare event

Part of the wonder of the Sea of Stars is **nobody knows exactly when** the plankton will glow. It usually happens in late summer, but it depends on the **climate** and the population of plankton.

Plankton

The world of the future

Our world is always changing. What do you think it will be like in the **future**? We don't know for sure what's going to happen, but it's up to us to make sure it changes for the better!

Living longer?

Doctors and scientists are working to invent new medicine and **cure diseases**. One day, humans may be able to live for hundreds of years!

By the year 2050, there will be almost

165 TODAY!

Robots already do jobs for us and they are becoming more intelligent. They may be a big part of our lives in the future.

Alien life

Some people believe there is life on other planets and that someday we will **find each other**. There's no proof of this, but imagine having an alien friend!

What about our planet?

The future of Earth is a worry. We need to **help save the planet** from climate change, pollution, deforestation, and other problems. Experts are working to fix these problems, but we need to do more.

We know very little about the oceans. It's likely we'll make amazing new discoveries soon.

Some astronauts already live in space on the International Space Station. Maybe we will be able to live on the Moon or another planet one day.

219

Index